Santa Barbara
Community Builders

Connecting Our Coastal Community

Michael Bowker

Published by BoehmGroup, Inc.

www.sbcommunitybuilders.com

Editor: Betsy Crist

Graphic Designer: Don French

Library of Congress Number: 2013933121

ISBN: 978-0-9850956-2-8

eBook ISBN: 978-0-9850956-3-5

Printed in China

Featured photographer: Scott Gibson
pages cover, 9, 11, 12-13, 24-25, 36-37, 46-51, 58-59, 60-63, 68,
74-77, 80-81, 100, 103-106, 109, 112-113, 120-121, 128

Santa Barbara Community Builders

Connecting Our Coastal Community

Michael Bowker

Table of Contents

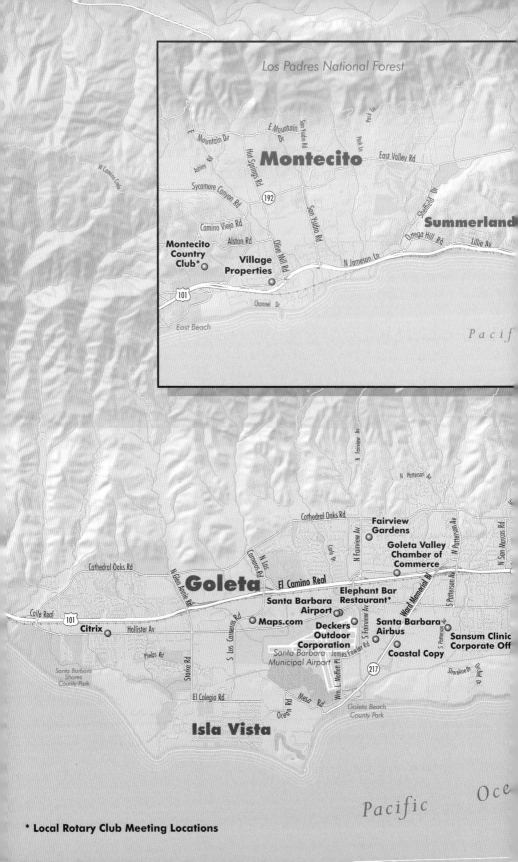

Los Padres National Forest

Montecito

Summerland

E Mountain Dr

E Mountain Dr

San Ysidro Rd

Park Ln

Park Ln

East Valley Rd

Ashley Rd

Hot Springs Rd

Sycamore Canyon Rd

192

San Ysidro Rd

Sheffield Dr

Camino Vieja Rd

Alston Rd

Olive Mill Rd

Ortega Hill Rd

Lillie Av

**Montecito
Country
Club***

**Village
Properties**

N Jameson Ln

W Camino Creek

101

Channel Dr

East Beach

Pacif

N Fairview Av

N Patterson Av

Cathedral Oaks Rd

**Fairview
Gardens**

N Fairview Av

Carla Dr

N Patterson Av

**Goleta Valley
Chamber of
Commerce**

N San Marcos Rd

N Los Carneros Rd

Cathedral Oaks Rd

Goleta

El Camino Real

**Elephant Bar
Restaurant***

Ward Memorial Bl

S Patterson Av

N Glen Annie Rd

Calle Real

101

Hollister Av

**Santa Barbara
Airport**

S Los Carneros Rd

Maps.com

**Deckers
Outdoor
Corporation**

S Fairview Av

**Santa Barbara
Airbus**

S Patterson Av

Citrix

Phelps Rd

Stoke Rd

Santa Barbara
Municipal Airport

James Fowler Rd

Wm. L Moffett Pl

217

Coastal Copy

Shoreline Dr

Ox Rd Rd

**Sansum Clinic
Corporate Off**

Santa Barbara
Shores
County Park

El Colegio Rd

Orcon Rd

Mesa Rd

Goleta Beach
County Park

Isla Vista

Pacific

Oce

* Local Rotary Club Meeting Locations

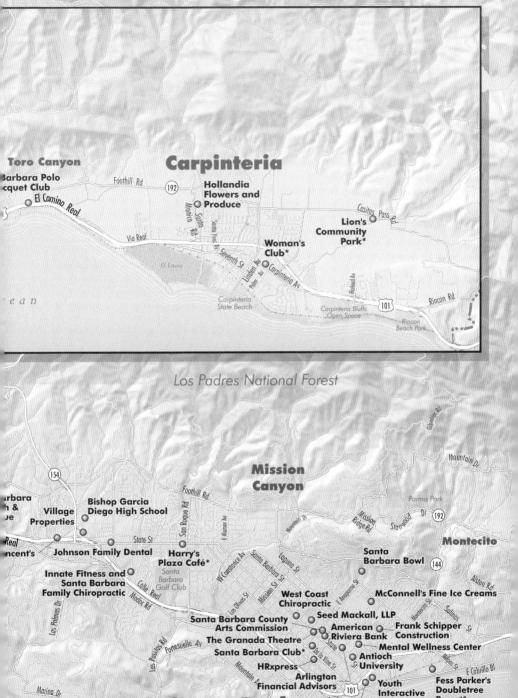

Toro Canyon

Barbara Polo
cquet Club

El Camino Real

Foothill Rd (192)

Carpinteria

**Hollandia
Flowers and
Produce**

Casitas Pass Rd

**Lion's
Community
Park***

Via Real

Santa Monica Rd

Santa Ynez Av

Seventh St

**Woman's
Club***

Linden Av

Palm Av

Carpinteria Av

El Estero

Ballard Av

Carpinteria
State Beach

Carpinteria Bluffs
Open Space

(101)

Rincon Rd

Rincon
Beach Park

ean

Los Padres National Forest

(154)

**Mission
Canyon**

Parma Park

arbara
h &
e

**Village
Properties**

**Bishop Garcia
Diego High School**

Foothill Rd

Mission
Ridge Rd

Starwood
Dr

(192)

Montecito

Real

ncent's

State St

San Roque Rd

E Alamar Av

Newton Dr

Johnson Family Dental

**Harry's
Plaza Café***

**Santa
Barbara Bowl**

(144)

**Innate Fitness and
Santa Barbara
Family Chiropractic**

Calle Real

Santa
Barbara
Golf Club

W Constance Av

Laguna St

Santa Barbara St

McConnell's Fine Ice Creams

Alston Rd

Modoc Rd

**West Coast
Chiropractic**

Los Olivos St

Mission St

E Anapamu St

Seed Mackall, LLP

**Frank Schipper
Construction**

Los Positas Rd

**Santa Barbara County
Arts Commission**

**American
Riviera Bank**

State

Mental Wellness Center

Portesuello Av

The Granada Theatre

Santa Barbara Club*

De la Vina St

**Antioch
University**

Mountain Rd

HRxpress

**Arlington
Financial Advisors**

(101)

**Youth
Interactive**

**Fess Parker's
Doubletree
Resort***

Marina Dr

Santa Barbara

Elings
Park

Cliff Dr

Cliff Dr

Meigs Rd

Loma Alta Dr

**Enterprise
Fish Company**

(225)

San Rafael Av

San Shoreline Dr

0   0.5   1 mile

©**MAPS**.com

Jeff, Eric, and Steve Boehm

Message From the Publisher

Doing business in the Santa Barbara area is a unique experience. It can be exhausting, competitive, and expensive, yet Santa Barbara is also one of the most rewarding places to work on the planet. This community is filled with dynamic, talented, and intriguing people. That's why I knew early on that there was a treasure trove of hidden gems scattered about the area—diamonds in the form of stories.

Operating under the belief that people want to know more about the organizations they support, we created a diverse collection of articles, each account a compelling glimpse into the heart of a local business. Our goal is to help the community get to know these businesses in a more meaningful way.

Words cannot express how grateful I am to my family for their support. Thank you to my partner in life, Ashley Doubleday, for her constant love and ongoing patience; to my dad, Steve Boehm, for support in sales and business strategy; and to my mom, Ingrid Boehm, for being totally awesome.

A special thank you is owed to my grandfather, Eric H. Boehm, for allowing me the opportunity to share in his vision—to promote story-telling in Santa Barbara. Eric is a role model of health, kindness, and generosity for us all.

And I also offer thanks to the team: first and foremost to Michael Bowker, for his skills and experience in interviewing and writing; to Don French, for his strong business ethics and beautiful graphic layouts; to Scott Gibson, for his breathtaking photographs; to editor Betsy Crist, for her attention to detail; and to Jennifer Brannon, for the lessons she's taught me over the years and for her undying positivity. Each one has given more than necessary to make this publication a possibility.

I am so proud to see this project blossom from a heartfelt idea to what I hope will be a lasting community publication. This book is a tribute to the efforts, tenacity, and achievements of all the Santa Barbara Community Builders.

Jeff Boehm
(805) 268-2528
jeff@sbcommunitybuilders.com

Introduction

Jeff Boehm has been my friend and fellow publishing aficionado since I arrived in Santa Barbara in 2008. When he asked me to write this book with him, I was delighted and said yes immediately. I have tremendous respect for Jeff and his entire family, including his grandfather, Eric Boehm.

Jeff's vision for this book was to create a way for you to better understand, in ways that perhaps you've never known them before, the businesses, nonprofits, and individuals that shape this community. Each profile is self-contained and personal. There is a little bit of everything in this book, from history and business philosophies to some compelling views on life and what community really means.

In the more than 60 interviews I conducted, everyone had something valuable to share. Much of it was inspiring, most of it was thought-provoking, and all of it was spiked with a sense of humor.

I always asked whether there were any public misconceptions about the company or brand. One of the quickest answers came from the spokesman for the Sansum Clinic who said, "Yes! Please tell people we are not a free clinic. We are more like the Mayo Clinic."

I don't think there was a single interview where we didn't share a laugh or two over something. Santa Barbarans have a great sense of humor, an abundance of vision and imagination, and a talent for getting things done.

In these pages, you'll learn why a sailing ship is featured on the Goleta Chamber of Commerce logo and what is behind Michael Towbes's remarkable devotion to the Granada Theatre. You'll also learn about the amazing rise of Deckers, Citrix, and other local world-conquering companies; the surprising histories of the Santa Barbara Bowl, the Polo Club, and St. Vincent's; and the inspiring entrepreneurial success stories of Dr. Nancy Leffert, Erik Onnen, Dr. Steven Johnson, Tom Rizk, and many other outstanding community builders.

In this book are the true and otherwise untold stories of the people who make the Santa Barbara region what it is, one of the best and most big-hearted places to live in the world.

Michael Bowker

About the Author

Michael Bowker lives in Santa Barbara and owns a literary company that specializes in writing and publishing memoirs, biographies, how-tos, and narrative nonfiction for clients. He is a best-selling author whose 16 books include Playing from the Heart *(Random House),* Fatal Deception *(Simon & Schuster),* The Visionary Leader *(Random House), and* Winning the Battle Within *(Kele Books). He has written more than 4,000 magazine articles, served as the senior speech writer for the mayor of Los Angeles, and served as executive editor of a national business magazine. His stories have been the basis of five television movies. He can be reached at mbowker@inreach.com.*

Butterfly Beach

Nonprofit Granada Theatre Is the Cultural Heart of Santa Barbara

I t is fitting that the Granada Theatre is housed in the tallest building in Santa Barbara. Everything about the Granada Theatre seems larger than life, from the legacy it is creating for Santa Barbara as one of the outstanding performing arts centers in the United States to its most generous benefactors, Anne and Michael Towbes, high-profile community leaders who have helped shaped the city for many decades.

The idea that Santa Barbara could build and support a world-renowned venue for cultural events was audacious, but the visionary individuals who came together in 1997 to form the Santa Barbara Center for the Performing Arts (SBCPA), the nonprofit organization that operates the theater, believed it could be done. Their decades-long search for a proper venue ultimately focused on the Granada

Theatre, which has a grand history of hosting such entertainers as Al Jolson, Charlie Chaplin, Fred Astaire, and Henry Fonda. Michael Towbes was a founding member of the SBCPA board of directors, which included a diverse group of community leaders who worked together tirelessly to raise the nearly $70 million that was needed to fully restore and modernize the Granada Theatre into the spectacular showcase it is today—a valued community asset that defines the spirit and culture of Santa Barbara.

In addition to operating the Granada Theatre, the SBCPA supports eight resident performing arts companies: the Santa Barbara Symphony, Opera Santa Barbara, the Santa Barbara Choral Society, the State Street Ballet, the Music Academy of the West, UCSB Arts & Lectures, Theater League, and the Community Arts Mu-

"Anne and Michael Towbes are passionately devoted to serving our community, and helping to restore the Granada Theatre as Santa Barbara's cultural center is at the top of their list of personal accomplishments." —Kristi Newton

sic Association. The Granada Theatre also presents the best of contemporary entertainers from around the world through the Granada Theatre Concert Series. The Granada Theatre does not receive financial support from the government and, like most world-class theaters, covers only half its annual budget through ticket sales and other earned income. This means that each year the Granada Theatre benefits from gifts and sponsorships to maintain the level of excellence in programming and operations that the community and the theater's exemplary resident companies expect.

Kristi Newton, director of development, leads SBCPA's fund-raising efforts for the benefit of the Granada Theatre and all of its resident companies. "The coming year is an important and exciting one for us—April of 2014 marks 90 years since the original opening of our town's historic Granada Theatre." she said. "We want the community to know the Granada Theatre is here for everyone to enjoy." About Towbes, Newton said: "Michael and Anne give much more than money; they invest an enormous amount of time and effort every year making sure we achieve our strategic goals. They share a passion and love for Santa Barbara, and for the Granada Theatre as our community's historic and vibrant pillar for the performing arts."

1214 State Street
Santa Barbara, CA 93101
(805) 899-2222
www.granadasb.org

Supporting a $124 Million Art and Cultural Industry

Santa Barbara County Arts Commission

Bob DeBris

"ART IS PART OF OUR EVERYDAY EXISTENCE IN SANTA BARBARA. I CAN'T IMAGINE THIS CITY WITHOUT IT."

From the free Summer Film Series in the Sunken Gardens to the Pianos on State Street and the annual countywide Arts Symposium, the Santa Barbara Arts Commission and its small but ambitious staff are a big part of what makes this region special. The Arts Commission, established in 1977, plays a major role in supporting Santa Barbara's $124 million art and cultural industry and promoting the region as a national art center.

"We have a passion for helping people appreciate what artists do," said Rita Ferri, visual arts coordinator. "We want to help share the beauty they create and help broaden people's view of what art is." Ferri and Ginny Brush, executive director, are the only two full-time staff. Along with one part-time staff member, these energetic and talented women conduct an astonishingly wide range of activities.

Ginny Brush

The Arts Commission administers the city's cultural grant programs, which help fund about 75 grassroots cultural nonprofits; helps regional artists find venues for exhibitions and performances; coordinates numerous school art outreach programs; and tirelessly promotes Santa Barbara County as an art and cultural tourist destination.

"People have the misconception that the arts cost the government money, but in fact, they contribute greatly to the economy of this area," said Brush. "We provide the technical support artists and nonprofits need to realize their vision and thrive." The Arts Commission serves as a catalyst for creating public/private partnerships to make the arts more accessible to the public.

The Arts Commission, which was the brainchild of then county supervisor Peter Stalker and artist Channing Peake, collaborates with dozens of local organizations, including the Santa Barbara Bowl and UCSB Arts and Lectures. It has public galleries in the County Administration Building, the City Hall in Santa Barbara, and the Betteravia Government Center in Santa Maria.

The future looks encouraging for the Arts Commission and the county's art and cultural community. "One of our goals is to help create an endowment for the restoration of our existing public art," said Ferri. "Art is part of our everyday existence in the Santa Barbara area. I can't imagine this region without it. Art makes life worth living."

1100 Anacapa Street
Santa Barbara, CA 93101
(805) 568-3990
www.sbartscommission.org

Opposite: The Arts Commission at the Leadership in the Arts Award Reception, 2011. Top: Pianos on State Street, 2011. Below: City Grant recipients with the mayor at Economic Impact of Arts & Cultural Tourism on Santa Barbara County, 2013.

Neil Campbell

$38 Million Raised to Restore City's Beloved Historic Venue

Despite its popularity, the Bowl still harbors an aura of intriguing mystery. Part of this is its hidden location off upper Milpas Street, and part comes from its relatively unknown and surprisingly long and varied history. Moreover, few people know that today it is run by a small staff and 21 dedicated volunteer board members. The Bowl has transformed into a state-of-the-art facility—some of the world's

Tucked into a beautiful ravine and hillside overlooking the city and the Pacific Ocean, the Santa Barbara Bowl helps define Santa Barbara and is a beloved, vital, and historic piece of the city's cultural fabric. This is a year of celebration for the proud musical landmark as it marks the successful achievement of the capital phase of a Herculean fund-raising effort—the American Classic Capital and Endowment Campaign—that began in 1994 and culminated last year with more than $38 million being raised for restoration and new projects.

The Bowl, which was showing its age with a cracked cement stage and deteriorating seating, received a complete overhaul beginning in 1995. What emerged from all these efforts is a 4,562-seat, world-class outdoor venue. More improvements are under way, including a new, park-like entrance that will allow vehicles and patrons to enter separately, but the Santa Barbara Bowl Foundation, which oversees the Bowl, is also shifting its focus to endowment for education outreach programs and a sustainable maintenance fund.

most popular musicians, including Norah Jones, Jack Johnson, and Gwen Stefani, play there frequently—but it was actually built 76 years ago as part of a federal government WPA project during the Great Depression. "The original work was done primarily by Italian and Mexican stonemasons, some 25 years before Carlos Santana, David Crosby, and Kenny Loggins [who have all played at the Bowl] may have picked up their first guitars," said Rick Boller, the youthful executive director of the foundation.

In the hallway under the stage and in backstage dressing rooms are photos that show the venue as it was in 1937—a bowl-shaped structure with a wooden stage at the bottom and seats rising up on all sides. The wooden stage revolved 360 degrees during performances and was built primar-

ily to house the dancing and musical finale of the Old Spanish Days Festival. Although revered for years, the Bowl fell into disrepair and dormancy during World War II and narrowly escaped demolition more than once during its history.

Nederlander Organization, one of the most prestigious operators of live theater, opera, and outdoor music venues in the world. Nederlander is a profit organization representing a unique partnership between the for-profit world, government agencies (the Bowl

There is "a lot of music yet to be played."

Today, more than 115,000 people flock to performances at the Bowl every year, and it would be hard to think of Santa Barbara without it. The Bowl itself is run by the Santa Barbara Bowl Foundation, a community-driven nonprofit organization that does not receive much funding from ticket sales. "The artists who perform at the Bowl are primarily the force behind setting the ticket prices to their shows," said Boller. "Not many people in Santa Barbara know that." The foundation has partnered for several years with the

land is owned by the county of Santa Barbara), and the Santa Barbara Bowl Foundation.

Eric Lassen, a Santa Barbara architect who has served on the board since its inception, has spent thousands of hours volunteering his considerable talents to the restoration of the facility. Lassen, who is currently the chair of the Facilities Committee, says it has been an effort of love. "I remember our first project in 1983. We were trying to figure out how to fund an irrigation system for a small

new lawn in the front," he said with a laugh. "That was the scale in those days. Our largest project cost $8 million. We've come a long way."

Lassen and the other members of the foundation plan to continue its highly successful outreach program, which benefits students throughout the county. The Bowl already commits $1 per ticket to help fund Santa Barbara County arts education programs, including a variety of programs for schools, teachers, students, nonprofit arts organizations, and venues. These outreach initiatives have distributed more than $750,000 for education in the past 10 years.

The foundation has also been renegotiating its lease with the county, which would give it an extension of 45 years with an option for another 25 years upon completion of the Facility Master Plan. "That will give us 70 years' security on the lease," said Lassen. "That's a lot of music yet to be played."

Lassen credits a number of dedicated local volunteers for the current success of the Bowl. "It was in pretty bad shape 25 years ago, but a lot of people came together to save it—and they are still at it," said Lassen, who still manages the major capital projects. He and others hired the original architects: Santa Barbara–based Design Arc and the New York firm Handel and Associates, who began sketching the current stage housing in 1994. "I'm constantly amazed at the cohesiveness of the people involved; they are the most skilled and talented group I've ever worked with," Lassen added. "On the Facility Committee, the same people have met every month for 20 years." The original architectural firms and construction contractors have also remained throughout the restoration, helping give the Bowl its overall consistent look and feel.

The future of the Bowl is brighter than ever. "We think this is the most beautiful premier arts venue on the West Coast," said Boller. "We have people who have attended the Bowl since the 1970s now dropping their kids off to see concerts; they are that comfortable with us. But, most of all, it is our dedicated volunteers and committed staff who saved it, and now make it all work. They are fantastic. We are all united by a love of this place."

1122 North Milpas Street
Santa Barbara, CA 93103
(805) 962-7411

Santa Barbara Harbor

Smooth Flying at Santa Barbara Airport

Plans to Add Future Flights

The Santa Barbara Airport (SBA) is a regional gem with a rich 80-year history and service to more than 720,000 passengers per year. The airport is a vital part of the economic fabric of the California central coast.

Since its inception, SBA has been a financially self-supported enterprise funded through tenant rents and user fees. Over the past 25 years the airport has received $108 million in Federal Aviation Administration (FAA) grants for airfield and aviation facility improvements that benefit the flying public. FAA grant funds are derived from the tax passengers pay on their airline tickets. "The airport is operated as much like a private company as any governmental entity can be," said Karen Ramsdell, airport director for the past 26 years.

Five major airlines (United Airlines, Frontier Airlines, American Eagle, US Airways, and Alaska Airlines) serve five nonstop destinations and hundreds of one-stop destinations throughout the world. Ramsdell said that one common misconception is that the airport is involved in setting

ticket prices and routes, which it does not. Thirty-four years ago Congress deregulated the airline industry, removing government control over fares, routes, and market entry.

Ramsdell is proud of the quality service the airport provides the region. "For a small airport to offer five major airlines that offer access to anywhere in the world is incredible. I'm not sure that people here realize that few cities our size have an airport of this quality." Currently, the longest nonstop flights are from Santa Barbara to Denver, offered by United and Frontier, and Santa Barbara to Seattle, offered by Alaska. This past summer the biggest news was the return of Alaska's SBA-PDX (Portland) nonstop during the summer season. This route was so successful that the airport expects the service to return in summer 2013, according to Ramsdell. "Passenger participation is critical to the success of keeping air service at the Santa Barbara Airport."

In addition to offering commercial airline flights, the Santa Barbara Airport also supports nearly 120 privately owned aircraft. General aviation aircraft, from small single-engine airplanes to large private jets, play an important role in the local economy by bringing in over a quarter of a million visitors to the region.

The airport has been owned and operated by the City of Santa Barbara since 1941. Originally, the city purchased 540 acres of airport property, which was then expanded to 952 acres after World War II when the federal government closed the Marine Corps Air Station and deeded an additional 412 acres to the city. In 1960, the city was successful in adding its airport property within the city limits by an innovative, although controversial, annexation that connected the airport property to the city via a 500-foot wide strip of land that runs along the ocean floor, according to Ramsdell.

The airport is a vital economic link in the regional economy, generating a direct and indirect impact of more than a half billion dollars, according to Ramsdell. Across the street from the airfield, the airport operates a 100-acre industrial park. The 100 businesses that lease space from the airport provide about 1,000 local jobs

and rental income that helps support the aviation activities. These non-aviation businesses include small tech companies, Twin Lakes Golf Course, the State Crime Lab, and building material companies. According to Ramsdell, the airport generates about $14 million in annual revenue, of which about $4.3 million comes from non-aviation sources.

The Santa Barbara Airport is also steward for the 430-acre Goleta Slough State Ecological Reserve adjacent to the airfield. The Goleta Slough is a coastal estuary that provides habitat for a vast array of wildlife, including endangered species. Since 1999, the airport has enhanced or restored more than 65 acres of wetland habitat. The airport staff includes a full-time environmental planner to handle the wetland issues. "We take our environmental responsibilities very seriously," Ramsdell said. "Many residents may not be aware that we do this, but it is a trust we keep for them."

In August 2011, the airport opened a new 72,000 square foot airline terminal. This improvement tripled the space available for passengers, airlines, concessionaires, and passenger screening. The result has been smoother and faster transitions through security for passengers. Once they are through the security line, passengers will find such amenities as food and beverage, news, and gift stands; restrooms; computer workstations; free Wi-Fi; and a comfortable waiting area. The completion of the new short-term parking lot has eased much of the congestion that occurred during the construction phase. A big plus at the terminal is the new ground transportation lane that allows cabs, buses, and limousines to have a lane of their own and not interfere with the flow of private vehicles picking up and dropping off passengers. "From passenger comments I think the expansion was very successful," said Ramsdell. "Some of our passengers miss the quaintness of the old terminal, but we arrived at a point where we couldn't continue to squeeze increasing numbers of passengers through a terminal that was built for half that number. There comes a time where safety, efficiency, and comfort become more important." On October 30, 2012, the City Council voted to name the new terminal building the John T. Rickard Terminal. The newly restored histor-

ic terminal is named for aviator Earle Ovington.

The Airport Department has 53 staff members under Ramsdell's direction. As the airport director, Ramsdell is responsible for over-all management of the airport and implements the policies set forth by the city administrator and the City Council. Airport staff provide support for the seven-member Airport Commission appointed by the City Council. Besides the Airport Department staff, 1,500 people are employed at the terminal by the airlines, rental car companies, the Transportation Security Administration, the FAA, and other private companies.

One of the biggest challenges that the airport faces is the constant stream of new security regulations and procedures, Ramsdell said. "Since 9/11, there have been hundreds of new security regulations. Keeping up with those is challenging, as they often require additional staffing and capital outlays. At the same time, we work very hard to keep the experience of passengers, private aircraft owners, and aviation businesses as positive as possible while complying with federal laws."

The future of the airport appears bright. "Once the airlines finish the current shakeout and the economy improves, we will begin to see an increase in air travel and a continued expansion in routes," said Ramsdell.

"Since its inception, the airport has been a financially self-supported enterprise."

"In the meantime, we will continue to serve the community to ensure that passengers have the best possible experience while they are here."

The Santa Barbara Airport has facilitated air transportation in our region for over 80 years. As a transportation hub it is an integral part of the local economy, and as an environmental steward it strives to lead by example.

www.flysba.com

Frank Schipper Construction Commits to Quality Building

"It's nice to go out to dinner in Santa Barbara and see a client who gives you a big hug because they are happy with the job we did."

The Frank Schipper Construction Company, founded in 1982, is remarkably versatile, working on everything from the Victoria Theater to the Sea Center on Stern's Wharf and the Asian Elephant Exhibit in the Santa Barbara Zoo.

"We do whatever is needed to serve our clients and the community," said Paul Wieckowski, president and COO. "We are totally dedicated to customer service and quality building."

The wide range of the company's restoration and renovation efforts encompasses the Lobero Theater, the Humanities Building on the SBCC campus, the Music Academy, and the historic adobe on Santa Cruz Island. Its biggest project to date was the construction of the $12.5 million Serenity House, a beautiful inpatient hospice facility.

Company founder Frank Schipper retired in 2011, and the company is currently being purchased by the employees. "Frank is still involved with the operation," said Wieckowski. "The way we do business won't change because we are still bound together by our core values and by the model Frank built. We pride ourselves on team effort, on the quality of our work, and by the fact that we stand behind everything we do. It's nice to go out to dinner in Santa Barbara and see a client who gives you a big hug because they are happy with the job we did."

"A misconception about the company is that we don't do small jobs," said Wieckowski, who has been with the company for 26 years. "That's simply not true. We even fix doors for people if that's what they need."

The company, which hopes to do $30 million in jobs this year, has won dozens of local and statewide awards, including two recent first-place awards from the Santa Barbara Contractors Association and the prestigious Excellence in Project Management Award from the Association of General Contractors of California for its work at the zoo. "We like finding innovative ways to solve challenges," said Wieckowski. "Most of all, we know that by working as a team and standing behind our work 100 percent, we can continue to succeed by serving this community."

610 East Cota Street
Santa Barbara, CA 93103
(805) 963-4359
www.schipperconstruction.com

VILLAGE PROPERTIES

Community Involvement Pays Off

W hen Renee Grubb and Ed Edick grew frustrated with working for the corporate-owned real estate firms that dominated the Santa Barbara landscape in 1996, they came up with an idea that was both risky and appealing.

Grubb and Edick were friends and had a similar outlook. After several months of coaxing by Grubb, Edick agreed to be a part of the launch of a local real estate company. The market was struggling at the time, and they didn't really know if any of the agents they knew would join them. At most, they thought they might be able to create a small boutique company. They called it Village Properties to reflect their local focus.

Grubb and Edick did not have to worry for long. Before the paint was dry in their new office on Coast Vilin Montecito, Santa Barbara, and Santa Ynez. The company services thousands of customers and has been able to give back more than a million dollars in charitable donations to local schools in the past 11 years.

"We were surprised by the level of our success, but looking back, it made sense because we've created exactly the type of company we, as agents, always wanted to work for," said Edick. "We based it on a culture of trust, caring, relationships, and community. I love walking through the front door of our offices every day because I truly like the people who are inside. We are very much like a family."

Being locally owned gives Village Properties some distinct advantages over its nationally based, corporate competitors. For example, community integration, a vital part of any real estate company's success, was easier for the firm because southern Santa Barbara County is the company's only focus. "It is where we commit all of our time and money," said Edick. "The nationwide companies can't do that because if they gave to our community, they would have to do the same for every community they serve. Their corporate headquarters is somewhere

lage Road, their phones began ringing off the hook. More than 20 of the top agents in town wanted to join the new company, which rocketed past the boutique stage in record time. "We opened our doors in May 1996, and we were in the black by the fourth quarter," said Grubb.

Today, Village Properties is a major player in the local real estate market, with more than 160 agents and offices

else, and they don't know and don't care as much about Santa Barbara." Becoming part of the community is vital because it allows agents to understand the needs and desires of area

"I love walking through the front door of our offices every day because I truly like the people who are inside. We are very much like a family."

residents, according to Grubb, who is a past president of the Santa Barbara Chamber of Commerce and is currently a trustee for the Santa Barbara Natural History Museum. "We listen and stay closely connected. People always ask us about the real estate market, so this community involvement is at the core of who we are and what we do."

Another focus of the company is service to its own agents, said Grubb. Having suffered through a corporate structure where they received little

assistance and had to drive to Los Angeles just to get training, Grubb and Edick make certain their agents are fully supported. "We work hard at being there for our agents," Grubb said. "We try to sustain a nurturing environment where loyalty is important. We have selected like-minded agents who value this and really want to be with us."

Staying on top of the latest advancements in technology is also a top priority. "Today, about 90 percent of people who are thinking of buying or selling a home use the Internet to help them," said Grubb. "We are out front in terms of constantly updating our Web site, using Twitter, Facebook, and all the other virtual tools that can help our clients. We maintain a personal touch while maximizing opportunities on the Web."

While the company is enjoying the resurgence in the housing market, for Grubb and Edick one of the most satisfying aspects of the Village Properties success story has been their ability to give back to the community.

They regularly sponsor the Santa Barbara Heart Walk's Kid's Zone, and the company also supports a wide variety of charities and community groups, including the United Way and Make-A-Wish foundations, the Santa Barbara Zoo, the Santa Barbara Museum of Art, the Museum of Natural History, and the Unity Shoppe.

The company's biggest community effort is the Village Properties Teacher's Fund, which has given more than $1 million to area schools. It is operated by the Village Properties Charitable Foundation. Much of the money is raised during an annual golf tournament sponsored by the company and supported by many community businesses. More than 1,700 classrooms in Santa Barbara County have benefited from the charity, which buys supplies, books, and other resources for the schools.

"Children are our future, and that's why we decided to devote much of our community support to the Teacher's Fund," said Edick. "It's been great for Renee and me to see the crazy idea

that we had 18 years ago not only serve our agents and clients but the students and teachers in our community. We never dreamed it would grow into something like this, but now that it has, we are focused on serving as many people as we can."

(805) 969-8900
www.villagesite.com

Santa Barbara County Courthouse

ANTIOCH UNIVERSITY

New Campus and Unique Partnership With SBCC Part of 'New Vision'

*A*ntioch University Santa Barbara (AUSB), which has been in Santa Barbara for 35 years, stepped into the community spotlight in 2012 when the campus moved to the corner of Cota and Anacapa streets, bringing new vitality to part of the downtown corridor.

AUSB offers bachelor's, master's, and doctoral programs, and has new leaders who are successfully promoting an exciting new vision for the school. This includes increased accessibility, an innovative agreement with Santa Barbara Community College (SBCC), and working partnerships with the city's business and nonprofit sectors, all of which are rapidly making the university a valued and increasingly recognizable community resource.

A nonprofit institution with a long, proud history of progressive education, the university welcomes students of all ages and ethnicities. Since its founding in Ohio in 1852, Antioch has promoted accessibility, social justice, and community involvement. Today, as more than 400 students attend classes at the new Santa Barbara campus, those traditions are still evident, and campus enrollment continues to grow.

"Accessibility is just the beginning for us," said university president Dr. Nancy Leffert. "Our mission is also connected directly to social justice and civic engagement. People come here because they want to 'make a difference' in the world." The school's demographics mirror that of the Santa Barbara population, Leffert said, with enrollment about 40 percent Hispanic.

For years, Antioch was a sleepy little satellite to the university's Los Angeles campus, but that changed in 2007, when Santa Barbara become an independent campus within the Antioch University system. A local board of trustees was established in 2009, and Leffert became AUSB's president in January 2011. Easygoing and with a quick sense of humor, she proved to be a decisive and confident leader. She began making changes and taking the school in a new direction. This included relocating the campus from its cramped quarters on Garden Street to the very visible and open new complex. Leffert credits Tom Parker, president and CEO of the Hutton Parker Foundation, which owns the complex, with making the move possible.

Intensive capital fund-raising provided for the needed renovation, and most of the work was completed on the new campus in the summer of 2012. "All the stars lined up in the right place for us," Leffert added.

The university's third bold move was to partner more closely with community colleges on the South Coast, particularly SBCC. "We developed a Bridge Program that provides students the opportunity to stay at SBCC for up to three years and then transfer

to Antioch, resulting in a cost-effective means of finishing their degrees," explained Leffert (pictured below on the left). The agreement guarantees SBCC students entrance into Antioch, as long as they satisfactorily complete designated courses at SBCC.

Antioch is thriving at a time when other universities are struggling. "We are working hard to serve our students, and we also have the advantage that many SBCC students don't want to leave Santa Barbara to finish college," Leffert said.

The mean age of students on the Antioch campus is 36 years old, and classes are often held at night and on weekends to serve employed students. "Sometimes it surprises people that we have such a mixture of ages in our classes," said Leffert. "We have traditional-aged students, and we also have 60-year-olds working to finish their bachelor's degrees. People

always ask me, 'What kind of environment does that create in the classrooms?' I tell them, 'A very rich one! Discussion among people of different ages provides a wonderful learning environment!'"

Antioch is a teaching university and therefore faculty focus on their students rather than on the demands of research. Classes are intentionally small, with a maximum of 25 students. Students receive narrative evaluations rather than traditional grades, and class discussions, writing, and critical thinking are the focus in all classes. The school has a relatively small staff, with much of the teaching done by adjunct faculty, which allows students the opportunity to learn from successful professionals within the community. The school emphasizes an "applied and experiential" approach to learning for students, meaning all students are required to

"A nonprofit institution with a long, proud history of progressive education, the university welcomes students of all ages and ethnicities."

work in the community in their field of study. The idea is for students to "take their education out into the community and then bring what they have learned back into the classroom," according to Leffert.

The university offers a bachelor of arts program in liberal studies with optional concentrations in applied psychology, business management and leadership, child development and education, communication and media, entrepreneurship, and environmental studies. Students can also earn a master of education via three teacher credential preparation programs, a master's in clinical psychology with concentrations in Latino/a mental health and healthy aging, and a doctorate in clinical psychology.

Leffert has helped build a campus culture that balances community involvement and practical learning skills and emphasizes intellectual and emotional growth. She is deeply committed to the students, as are the faculty and the board of trustees.

"Our future goals are to increase access to education and develop new programs relevant to Santa Barbara," said Leffert. "We have an advantage that we are not such a big university that we cannot change fairly quickly. We are flexible and nimble, and consequently, we can be more responsive to the changing educational and community needs. That's what makes this so exciting."

Examples of this can be found in the new programs being launched in 2013. AUSB will launch an MBA program, focusing on social business, nonprofit management, and strategic leadership, important elements in the Santa Barbara landscape. The Women & Leadership Certificate Program is aimed at helping women advance in the nonprofit, business, and public service sectors. The university is also scheduled to hold a week-long intensive Summer Writing Institute, which will likely be an annual event.

Antioch is making its mark on Santa Barbara, and the community is better off for it.

602 Anacapa Street
Santa Barbara, CA 93101
(805) 962-8179
www.antiochsb.edu

Community Rallies to Raise Endowment Funds

BISHOP GARCIA DIEGO HIGH SCHOOL

In 2005, a ripple of worry went through the community of parents whose children were attending Bishop Garcia Diego High School in Santa Barbara. The school had been operating since 1959, but it seemed that funding for the private Catholic school was dwindling.

"The campus was deteriorating," recalled David Borgatello, who had served for years on a school advisory committee and was a member of the school's first graduating class in 1960.

"It seemed that our money was going south to the Los Angeles Archdiocese, which ran the school, and people here were reluctant to donate because they were unsure if the funds would go directly to support the school."

Borgatello, who currently serves as vice president of Marborg Industries in Santa Barbara, and a handful of other school supporters decided to make a bold move. They elected to become an independent not-for-profit Catholic high school in 2005, and the school was suddenly on its own.

It survived, thanks to the efforts of the entire community, but with special contributions from Father Thomas Elewaut, John Gherini, Ralph Iannelli, Peter DaRos, and Keith Berry. Also notable in this critical transition were the efforts of Carla O'Neill; Catherine Boeddeker and her late husband, Ron Boeddeker; Dr. David Medina; and David Perry. Local architect Ed Lenvick designed a beautiful new gym, and most of the campus was renovated. Today, every teacher now has a teaching credential, and the 270 students have a clean, safe learning environment. Bishop is open to students of all religious beliefs.

"We work hard daily to instill in our students core values for life and prepare them for acceptance to our nation's best colleges and universities," said Dr. Paul Harrington, head of school. "We have advanced technology and small class sizes; students know we really care about them."

Borgatello's three daughters attended Bishop, as did his brother, Mario, and Mario's four children and two grandchildren. More grandchildren of both brothers will soon attend. "We have a vested interest in this school that goes back more than 50 years," said Borgatello with a smile. "I would say the future looks brighter than ever."

Plans include a campaign to raise funds for a permanent financial endowment. In addition, the school continues its Adopt-a-Student Program for financial assistance through an annual auction on the school grounds.

"THE FUTURE LOOKS BRIGHTER THAN EVER!"

"Our students know that nobody here will ever give up on them," said Harrington. "We could never have reached this point without David [Borgatello] and the other members of the board who were willing to take a risk. They made it work, and the students, parents, and entire community have benefited."

4000 La Colina Road
Santa Barbara, CA 93110
(805) 967-1266
www.bishopdiego.org

After 35 Years of Serving Great Food,
ENTERPRISE FISH COMPANY
Is a Santa Barbara Favorite

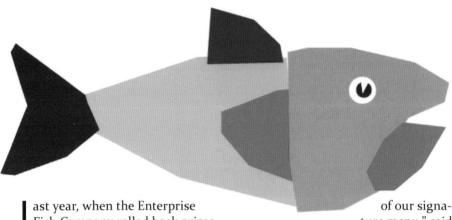

Last year, when the Enterprise Fish Company rolled back prices to celebrate 35 years of serving Santa Barbara some of the best seafood on the South Coast, people stormed the doors of the building with its familiar smokestack trademark. It was the culmination of decades of dedication, hard work, and an early financial gamble by the cofounders, Michael Bank and Randy LaFerr.

"It is wonderful to see," said Bank. "We were almost overwhelmed by the number of people who came in to help us celebrate. It's nice to know that we are a part of the fabric of Santa Barbara."

The continued success of the friendly restaurant and bar on lower State Street is based on the consistent quality of the food and service and its highly popular happy hour. "Our lobster specials on Monday through Thursday nights are a popular part of our signature menu," said Bank. "We serve a two-pound Maine lobster for $29.95, and people really love it." Executive chef Bruce Choi is also known for superb and innovative salmon dishes and other seafood and American cuisine offerings.

Happy hour draws locals and visitors alike in a cacophony of conversation, laughter, and clinking glasses. Televisions line the walls, so ball games are always easy to catch.

Bank and LaFerr opened the restaurant not long after graduating from UCSB, but they soon split with their financial partner, who took over the restaurant, while they assumed ownership of a second restaurant in Santa Monica. In 1991, Bank and LaFerr took a gamble and repurchased the now struggling original restaurant and added a partner, Michael Schmidtchen. Great food, friendly service, and a rocking happy hour brought everybody back to the old brick building, former home of the Enterprise Laundry, which serviced local area hotels. Bank and Laferr honored that era of Santa Barbara's history by keeping the Enterprise name.

"We are working toward a totally sustainable menu, and we hope to continue to present new and exciting menu offerings, but most of all we'll just keep making this a place where people can feel at home and get great seafood," said Bank.

225 State Street
Santa Barbara, CA 93101
(805) 962-3313
www.enterprisefishco.com

"Our lobster specials on Monday through Thursday nights are a popular part of our signature menu."

FAIRVIEW

GARDENS

Organic Teaching Farm Helps Community Return to its Roots

When children attend camp at the organic Fairview Gardens in Goleta, it isn't unusual for them to exclaim in wonder: "Wow! Carrots come out of the ground?" As a center for urban agriculture in the Santa Barbara region, the 12.5-acre farm and teaching facility on north Fairview Avenue is playing a crucial role in helping the community reconnect to the land and learn about farming, sustainability, and the environment. More than 10,000 people visit the farm annually to learn about their roots, literally and figuratively.

Fairview Gardens provides about 20 adult classes and suburban home-steading programs each year, ranging from how to grow an organic garden to how to make cheese. It is one of the oldest, most vibrant, and most popular organic teaching farms in the country.

"Demonstrating how we can be sustainable on a small-scale organic farm is part of our mission," said Mark Tollefson, the articulate and energetic center three years ago. "But the truth is, we've flunked organic agriculture. We're trying to change that."

The area was once a part of the largest Chumash Indian settlement on the coast, and the history of agriculture in the north Fairview area dates to 1895, when the Hollister family built the original house and began growing crops. It allegedly got its name one morning when Mrs. Hollister

executive director of Fairview Gardens. "We also grow and sell organic crops at farmers' markets, help interns and apprentices learn how to farm sustainably, and act as a community center in a variety of ways."

Tollefson sees Fairview Gardens as part of an effort to reverse current agricultural methods in the United States and around the world that he believes are unsustainable. "We've been talking about sustainability since the hippies first came on the scene in the late 1960s," said Tollefson, who assumed leadership of the exclaimed over the "fair view." Under her feet was some of the richest agricultural soil in California. At the time, citrus and walnut groves stretched to the ocean. The modern era began in the mid-1970s, when Roger Chapman, a professor of music, bought the property and named it Fairview Gardens. The land was carefully cultivated and nourished, and sunflowers flourished over the entire property. When the plants flowered, it was not unusual to see dozens of cars parked along the avenue as people stopped to photograph the stunning array.

Tollefson grew up on a farm in Canada and worked as a wilderness survival trainer before marrying San Diego native Sharon Tollefson, the education director at the center. "Sharon is the heart and soul of our teaching mission," he said. "Education is the key. We consider this an education center that happens to also be a farm." He also credits Julie Beaumont, director of farm operations, and Cesar

know they are most welcome here, and that this is their resource. If you have any questions on organic farming or sustainable agriculture, we will help you and give you every kind of support we can. We invite everyone to visit us. We have picnic tables all over the property, and anyone can come in and use them."

The property is also open to the public for weddings, festivals, or

Gomez, lead field hand, for their roles in the center's success.

The nonprofit center, which is governed by nine elected board members, collects some revenue from crops, classes, and other uses of the land but must rely on public donations to meet annual costs. Although past management of the center chose a more exclusive path, Tollefson is working hard to reach out to the community and rebuild relationships. "We have a new spirit of community and new goals," said Tollefson. "I want people in the Santa Barbara region and beyond to

other functions. Education remains the focus, however, and classes are increasing. The adult Suburban Homesteading programs begin in April and include the highly popular Introduction to Beekeeping and Harvesting Honey classes. Gardening classes include Get Your Green On, which covers spring and fall gardens. A Backyard Chickens series explores the process of raising chickens for food, and a Home Made Skills series presents such classes as Wild Fermenting and Soap Making Basics. Starting in early June, the Preserving the Harvest classes include Jams and Jellies, Canning Pickles, Peaches and Fruit, Tomatoes and Veggies and Apples: Sauce to Pies.

The extensive student programs include summer camps offering hands-on farming for young people, harvesting, games, experiments, and organic eating. After-school programs are also offered. "Students love doing real work on the farm, where they can touch the animals or the seeds and soil," said Tollefson. "My five-year-old son came out with me and helped plant an orchard. He kept asking me for things to do. Families love being out here together. Nobody is forced to learn; they really want to learn."

The student summer camps are held from mid-June through mid-August and are centered on real farm life. Three age groups run wild on the farm during the summer camps. Turnip Tots is the program for three- to five-year-olds, Pumpkin Pals is the program for six- to eight-year-olds, and Broccoli Bandits is the offering for nine- to eleven-year-olds. All programs focus on stewardship, connection to the land and nature, and unstructured play time balanced carefully with deep meaningful lessons based on real farm activities. Campers play in the worm bin, harvest food from the kids' garden, explore the richness of nature on the farm, and use the farm as a big canvas for arts and crafts.

Teens are encouraged to come and help as counselors in training during summer and after-school programs. Everyone learns together and grows from the experience on the farm.

As a working farm, Fairview Gardens produces more than 60 types of organic fruit and vegetables, which are sold in the Saturday farmers' markets in Santa Barbara, Goleta, and Santa Monica. A roadside stand will also be finished this year off Fairview Avenue that will offer produce from other organic farmers, according to Tollefson.

"We mimic natural systems in our diversity of produce," Tollefson said. "Too often, agricultural practices include planting huge fields with just one crop. This lack of diversity makes those fields highly vulnerable to bugs and other threats, giving rise to the need for insecticides and other harmful chemicals. We are showing it doesn't have to be done that way."

Although Fairview Gardens has undergone a shift in management direction under Tollefson, he praises the vision of the Chapman family and a small group of committed activists who bought the property and formed the nonprofit organization in 1994. Under the guidance of farm manager Michael Ableman, they placed it in trust with the Land Trust for Santa Barbara County and transformed it into an early model for sustainable, organic, urban agriculture.

Much of the future of Fairview Gardens now lies with Tollefson and his team, whose passion and energy for the farm are easy to see. "One of the most enjoyable parts of this is getting the students out and connecting them to this natural process," he said. "Sometimes people give us a blank stare and ask why we want to do that. Spending time in this special environment, where you can see and learn how to grow your own food, has a profound and deeply influential effect. As Fukuoka said, 'The ultimate goal of farming is not the growing of crops, but the cultivation and perfection of human beings.'"

598 North Fairview Avenue
Goleta, CA 93117
(805) 967-7369
www.fairviewgardens.org

"We consider this an education center that happens to also be a farm."

A Labor of Love in Carpinteria
Hollandia Flowers and Produce

ollandia Flowers and Produce, LLC, has called the Carpinteria Valley home since 1970. The family business and products, especially its world-famous butter lettuce, have grown and prospered with Art and Magda Overgaag and their children, Leo, Ellen, Pete, and Karin, making Hollandia what it is today.

"My parents grew up in Holland, where their families had raised vegetables and flowers for generations," said Pete Overgaag, who helps manage the company. "In 1968, my father looked all over the world for the best growing climate, and he chose

Carpinteria. I think all of us are happy that he did!"

Today, Hollandia grows upland cress, avocados, cherimoyas, and their Living Butter Lettuce, which is marketed as Live Gourmet. More than 75 employees, who enjoy 401K retirement plans and health care coverage, grow and harvest the crops in rows of greenhouses off Santa Monica Road.

"When people think of agriculture, they often think of difficult work conditions and minimum-wage jobs," said Overgaag. "That isn't the case here. Our employees see this work as a career, and everyone comes together

Living
3-In-1 Lettuce
Absolutely Fresh Because It's Still Alive!

Living
Upland Cress
Absolutely Fresh Because It's Still Alive!

Living
Red Butter Lettuce
Absolutely Fresh Because It's Still Alive!

Living
Butter Lettuce
Absolutely Fresh Because It's Still Alive!

with great attitudes. It is an enjoyable work environment, and we move forward as a team."

The four types of lettuce and leafy greens are grown hydroponically in state-of-the-art greenhouses where the company maintains one of the cleanest growing environments in agriculture. Weed abatement, production-area hygiene, and pest-control measures, bolstered by the physical barrier of the greenhouse, help limit chances of product adulteration, according to Overgaag.

Employees receive extensive training in food safety and production. Quality assurance is provided through third-party inspections by independent certified laboratories and intensive internal audits.

The company's "Absolutely fresh because it's still alive" promise is enjoyed by millions of Americans every year. The products are sold to grocery stores, specialty shops, wholesalers, hotels, and restaurants throughout the South Coast.

The company prides itself in being "clean and green." "We're always researching new, clean technology to increase our quality and efficiency," said Overgaag. "For our family and employees, working here is a labor of love."

info@livegourmet.com
www.livegourmet.com

"In 1968, my father looked all over the world for the best growing climate, and he chose Carpinteria. I think all of us are happy that he did!"

McConnell's
FINE ICE CREAMS
A 70-year-old, sweet Santa Barbara legacy

Since 1949

McConnell's

ice cream

Back in 1949, Gordon "Mac" McConnell and his wife, Ernesteen, had a dream: to make the best ice cream in the world. And ever since, Santa Barbara's legendary McConnell's Fine Ice Creams has been churning out some of the country's finest, hand-crafted scoops of delight.

Today, under McConnell's new owners, husband and wife Michael Palmer and Eva Ein, McConnell's forges ahead, as strong as ever.

"McConnell's is one of the country's oldest, continually operating creameries. "We make the ice cream the same way Mac made it 70 years ago. From scratch. We set our standards very high, but we never forget to have fun along the way. This is Santa Barbara, after all."

The Ein-Palmers, who purchased the creamery from former owner Jim McCoy (who passed away in early 2013) bring an array of talent, experience, and energy to McConnell's. Eva, a chef and restaurateur, is the long-time co-owner of two successful Santa Barbara restaurants. Michael is a winemaker and former brand communications and marketing executive. Their combined passions are food, wine, and, coincidentally enough, ice cream.

Together with McConnell's operations chief, Charley Price—a three-decade veteran of the dairy and ice cream business—the couple has invested their time, money, and heart into further developing McConnell's Fine Ice Creams' reputation as a world-class product.

"We're a small company, but we have big dreams," said Palmer, who grew up in Southern California and has fond memories of visiting Santa Barbara and enjoying McConnell's as a child.

When their house burned down in the 2008 Tea Fire, he and Ein spent time reevaluating their lives, ultimately deciding to invest in McConnell's rather than rebuild their home.

"Losing our home like that was a call of sorts. We wanted to spend our lives doing something different than what we were doing before. To do something we cared about. That was about bringing joy to ourselves and others. We knew it'd be hard work, and it has been. And it's a risk. And sometimes it's been frustrating, absolutely. But producing a product that people love—it turns out it's pretty fulfilling."

The McConnell's creamery is located at the Old Dairy, off Milpas Street, on East Canon Perdido, under the big cow that has kept watch over

that part of town for decades. The dairy was built in 1935 and has been a functioning creamery since then. The new owners have made a number of significant improvements to the plant, making it a clean and highly efficient mix of cutting-edge machinery, mixed with some of the original and classic equipment designed and built by Mac McConnell himself.

Supervising the process is Mike Vierra, one of the few master ice cream makers in the country. Vierra has been in residence at McConnell's for 35 years. A graduate of the dairy program at Cal Poly, Vierra is a perfectionist whose focus has never wavered from making the best ice cream in the world. "He really knows what he is doing," said Palmer. "He was hand-picked from one of the best dairy programs in the country by Jim McCoy all those years ago, and he's been here since.

> ## "The best ice cream in the world, as anyone who has tried it will argue, is sold by McConnell's of Santa Barbara"
>
> —*Time Magazine*

His knowledge and skills are second to none."

McConnell's, which has always been a family business, had an unlikely origin in World War II. "Mac was an Army pilot stationed in Europe during the war. While in France he sampled the ice cream" and thought it was the best he'd ever tasted. He researched their manufacturing methods—notably the "French pot process"—and schooled himself on their recipes and ingredients. Upon his return to America, "he built his own hopped-up, mechanized version of the process, combined it with the best ingredients, and went to town. Everybody loved it from the start," said Palmer.

McConnell built the company on his firm belief that his ice cream had to be the finest—the creamiest, densest, best-tasting in the business. Palmer,

Ein, and Price have kept that tradition, while adding their own values.

"We're a truly handcrafted product, from pasteurizing our own Central Coast milk and cream to crafting each one of our uniquely indulgent recipes, using the finest ingredients, from organic eggs and fruit, whenever possible, to the best chocolate and vanilla from multi-decade partners like Guittard and R. R. Lochhead. And McConnell's is one of the only companies in the business that uses absolutely no stabilizers whatsoever. Never had 'em. Never will."

Palmer and Ein are active in environmental and social issues in the community, but their focus is mostly on building the business right now. Ein recently developed several new flavors, including some that have become instant favorites (her salted caramel chip has already achieved legendary status). The future may include expanding to new products, and perhaps even the opening of new McConnell's-branded scoop shops, according to Palmer. "We're dreamers," he said. "Look. There are some good ice creams out there. Companies that do one or two things well.

Good ingredients or high butterfat or low overrun (low air). But finding a company that does all those things right? That produces a truly balanced product that excels on all fronts? That's tricky. That's what we obsess over. And I think we do a pretty good job of it."

McConnell's Fine Ice Creams is a California original, a cultural institution, a historic company that has never compromised.

"I want to make the world aware of how good this ice cream really is," Palmer said. "It's gonna take time, energy, and luck to get there, but I'm hopeful."

McConnell's currently offers 18 flavors in pints, five-ounce singles, five-liter gelato trays, and three-gallon tubs for food service and scoop shops. It is also available in hundreds of food markets and restaurants in Santa Barbara, Southern California, and throughout much of the western United States.

201 West Mission Street
Santa Barbara, CA 93101
(805) 569-2323
www.mcconnells.com

Along the Santa Barbara shore

A Family Affair for Health

When Andrew Azara was asked to describe the unique business combination he and his chiropractor brother, Dr. Nick Azara, offer in Santa Barbara, he said, "A holistic program that helps people successfully transform their health and fitness." While Nick offers family chiropractic services at Santa Barbara Family Chiropractic, Andrew, located at CrossFit Innate, an office and fitness center next door, conducts extensive functional fitness for individuals and groups. Together, the brothers help clients rebuild their bodies; eliminate muscular and joint pain; learn about healthy eating; and establish a customized, natural-movement fitness program aimed at achieving maximum mental and physical health.

Dr. Nick Azara

Andrew Azara

"Most people wait for a health crisis and then try to deal with it," said Nick. "Our combined programs help people build a healthy, sustainable lifestyle that heals the body and prevents physical and mental issues from arising. We view health as the keystone to vibrant families and communities. It's our goal to help people get the most out of life."

Nick, who opened his practice in 2011, provides a complete array of chiropractic services, from thorough joint, muscle, and movement exams to adjustments and lifestyle consultations. His focus is on the health of families throughout Santa Barbara and the surrounding communities. His wife, Jen, plays a key role in helping to run the business. Nick, a graduate of UCSB, provides state-of-the-art, thorough, specific, and science-based evaluations. He uses high-tech imaging techniques and conducts multiple assessments.

"I don't adjust anyone until I do a complete evaluation and talk extensively to the client to see what his or her goals are. The adjustments are always safe and corrective based," said Nick. He added that even kids and infants should be checked regularly by a chiropractor. "I even adjust infants by hand, so the procedure is virtually painless, and it can prevent a host of problems later in life."

Although his methods and instruments are technologically advanced, Nick's approach is holistic, involving both body and mind in an effort to promote maximum health. "It all blends together," he said. "We help clients make better decisions about their health."

Andrew, also a UCSB graduate, has been a leading fitness coach in Santa Barbara for the past five years. Clients come to Nick in pain, and then Andrew and the team guide them to maximum strength and fitness after the pain is gone. Tall and fit like his brother, Andrew emphasizes "functional fitness" in his workout. "What our programs do is help people build their physical strength and movement in ways that are safe and important in daily life," he said. "We work on the strength, coordination, agility, and flexibility you need to do everyday things, and to enjoy the things you love to do much more."

Two other former UCSB students, Casey Pfeifer and China Cisney, helped cofound CrossFit Innate, and

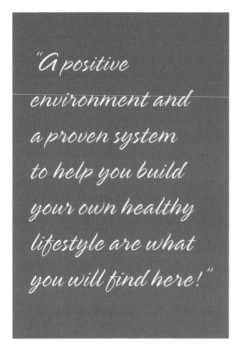

"A positive environment and a proven system to help you build your own healthy lifestyle are what you will find here!"

both act as fitness coaches. "They are both so smart, energetic, and have been an integral part of creating a quality program and a wonderful community. I feel very lucky to be working with them."

Working with families in the community is a specialty of the brothers. "We realize that when moms and dads get healthy, it makes a huge impact on the rest of the family and the whole community," said Andrew.

Healthy weight loss and body composition is another specialty. "You can lose weight through fad diets and drastic measures, but that usually doesn't last long," said Nick. "If you learn to eat right, exercise, and get adjusted, you will sleep better, gain far more energy for your day, and maintain an optimal weight while you work towards getting stronger and healthier every day."

Clients include people in all age groups, from infants to people in their 80s, who need chiropractic care and want to stay fit. "We meet you where you're at and help you get where you want to be," said Andrew. "Whether you're an experienced athlete or working with pain and injury, we help you work towards your goals safely and effectively. We push you, but we make it fun and achievable."

The Family Chiropractic and Fitness Center has become a community of its own. "We're brothers, and it makes such a huge difference to have a supportive community of coaches, friends, and family around participating and sharing the benefits." A common interest in better health draws people together.

"There are a lot of friendships made here," said Andrew. "Each week you can see the increased health in their energy and smiles. They come to us in pain and become stronger than they have been in their lives. A positive environment and a proven system to help you build your own healthy lifestyle are what you will find here!"

Innate Fitness
360 South Hope Avenue
Suite C-105
Santa Barbara, CA 93105
(805) 698-4057
www.innatebodybootcamp.com

Santa Barbara Family Chiropractic
360 South Hope Avenue
Suite C-100
Santa Barbara, CA 93105
(805) 682-4620
www.santabarbarafamilychiropractic.com

Setting New Standards for Dental Care

One of Dr. Steven Johnson's favorite sayings is "A smile can change a life." This belief motivated him to provide state-of-the-art, affordable, and painless dental care.

"I feel lucky to be able to play a role like this, where what you do can make a difference in people's health and in their lives," said Johnson. His three dental centers, including the new 5,400-square-foot head-quarters in Santa Barba-ra, service more than 120 patients per day, more than any private dental practice in the county.

Johnson Family Dental employs more than 65 people, including seven dentists and six hygien-ists in its high-tech head-quarters alone. The new building on State and La Cumbre features an array of high-tech laboratory equipment, which can do things like manufacture same-day crowns, as well as the latest imaging machines, which expose pa-tients to only one-tenth the radiation as traditional x-rays.

JOHNSON
FAMILY DENTAL

Johnson's "service first" attitude permeates the entire company and has manifested itself in one of the more successful business models on the South Coast. Since he purchased his father's practice in 2000, Johnson has pioneered a number of ways in which to better serve his patients.

"This is a fun dental center!" said Mary Madden, operations manager. "It is [fun] for the people who work here and for our patients." She attributes that to Johnson's contagious passion for his work. She added, "Our patients are greeted at the door with juice, cookies, and apples, and they know they are going to be treated by some of the best-trained dentists anywhere and serviced by the most up-to-date technology. People actually look forward to coming in here, knowing it is a peaceful, friendly atmosphere where their dental health is in great hands."

Jim Bartsch

Working with Johnson on the management team at the center are Madden; Nicole Clark, marketing director; and Frank Hovey, business manager. Johnson says this team is a major reason the center won the 2011 Best Dentist in Santa Barbara award from the city's magazine and was a finalist for the award in 2012.

Johnson Family Dental was one of the first medical centers to offer a free exam and x-rays to new patients. "That's a big part of our philosophy," said Johnson. "We think everybody should have access to a basic diagnosis. In today's economy, not everyone can afford even that." The center also offers some of the most advanced procedures available, including porcelain veneers, Invisalign braces, dental implants, pain-free root canals, tooth-colored fillings, dentures and partial dentures, and sedation dentistry.

The Johnson heritage in dental medicine in Santa Barbara goes back 50 years, when Dr. Gary Johnson, Steven's father, opened a practice on Fairview Avenue. After Steven graduated from dental school at the University of the Pacific in 1994, he practiced

"This is a fun dental center!"

with his dad. "The six years I worked with and learned from my father were among the best years of my life," he said. "He thought helping people through dentistry was pretty cool, and I share his feelings. He taught me that if I wanted to keep doing it, I had to build a business model that could adapt and grow in all economic times."

Listening to what patients want is the heart of the model. This included opening offices at 88 North Oak Street in Ventura and 678 Alamo Pin-

tado Road in Solvang in 2007. After outgrowing his old offices in Santa Barbara, Johnson built the new center, which includes a spacious, quiet waiting room featuring a beautiful wall of stacked stone; treatment rooms equipped with televisions for the patient's convenience; an employee learning center; and lab rooms where crowns are milled, images enlarged, and equipment sterilized.

Community involvement remains a critical part of Johnson's business and personal philosophy and sets him apart from other dentists. "There are many reasons for giving back to the community," he said. "There is the obvious one that it is the right thing to do, but we also think that we are in a position of helping to educate people on the importance of dental care, especially children, so they can begin to build positive lifelong habits."

For the past 10 years, the center has conducted a one-day "Dentistry With Love" program, where free cleanings, extractions, and fillings are offered. Hundreds of patients are seen on

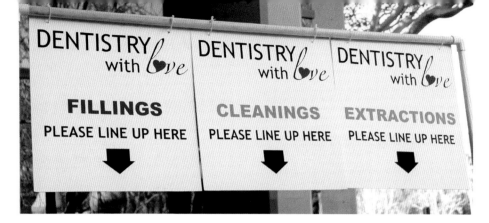

those days. A similar free program for children under 12 years old, "Little Hearts, Big Smiles," is scheduled in late summer. The staff dresses up in costumes, games are provided in the waiting room, and the children receive certificates of participation. The practice also offers periodic free seminars on such topics as dental implants and sleep apnea. Also, each year the staff donates to the Unity Shoppe, a nonprofit food bank that helps thousands of families in Santa Barbara County.

Perhaps closest to his heart, however, is the work Johnson and his staff do year-round for the Juvenile Diabetes Research Foundation (JDRF). His son, Braxton, 13, was diagnosed with type 1 diabetes four years ago, and Johnson is devoted to fighting the disease. The center donated $35,000 to JDRF, and in 2011 and 2012, Johnson served as the Tri-County JDRF corporate chairman and the Community Walk chairman.

The management team works hard to foster a positive work culture. "One thing we are excited about is our new Dental Assistant School, where we train people how to handle all the responsibilities that assistants have," said Johnson. The in-house learning center is just one way the company supports employee growth. An employee summit is held every year, and new ideas and concepts are encouraged from the staff.

Johnson continues to practice dentistry, while setting aside time for management oversight and his family. "I learned from my father that if you hire great people and let them take care of things, you can free yourself up to do what is most important to you," he said. "It's the same with patients. If you take care of them, they will take care of you. It's win-win; it works for everybody. I've never forgotten that."

3906 State Street, Suite 102
Santa Barbara, CA 93105
(805) 687-6767
www.johnsonfamilydental.com

ParentEd Offers Expert Guidance to Those Raising Children from Birth Through Adolescence

Dr. Marlene Roberts

Dr. Marlene Roberts (Dr. Mimi to her young clients) opened her new practice, ParentEd, in Montecito earlier this year. She does not define herself as a traditional clinical psychologist, however. Rather, she offers well-defined educational services to those interested in the psychological and physical growth and maturation of children. Sessions are highly specialized and individually driven, yet Roberts always begins by teaching clients the basics of positive communication and self-talk. "In the young child, I use the analogy of a little bird that whispers a message of empowerment and esteem," Roberts stated.

"I love educating expectant parents pre- and post-delivery or [before] adoption of a child. Relationships have a better chance at evolving in healthy ways when couples know what to expect."

Roberts learned resilience and the practical side of parenting from her parents, who raised Roberts and her three siblings with optimism and faith as a baseline, and by raising four children of her own, Zachary, William, Morgan, and Michelle.

In 2005, she was given the prestigious Humanism Award by the directors of the UCLA Medical Center for her innovative work in nursing excellence. When working with the adolescent population, Roberts stated, "I teach parents how to set standards while showing love, and most of all, how to communicate with a non-communicative child."

Roberts is a registered nurse with more than 25 years' experience. She said, "the power of positive thinking and positive self-talk were key in the decision to earn a doctorate in clinical psychology at the age of 45."

She used many of the positive-thinking techniques she teaches to overcome her severe fear of swimming in the ocean. Last year she competed successfully in six triathlons, including the Santa Barbara event, which included a half-mile ocean swim. This year she has qualified for the USA Triathlon National Championships after finishing in the top 10 percent of her age group in two triathlons.

"There is a sense of empowerment and joy that comes from learning to communicate positively with oneself," Roberts said. "I love sharing these techniques with people."

(562) 310-3455

"In the young child, I use the analogy of a little bird whispering a message of empowerment and esteem."

sansum^{SM}
CLINIC
for your good health

World-Class Health Care in a Team Environment

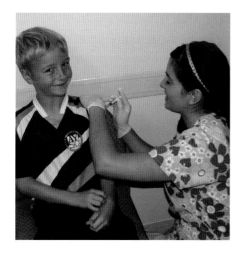

More than 150,000 patients, from Santa Barbara and around the world, are seen at Sansum Clinic every year, making it the largest independent, nonprofit medical center between Los Angeles and San Francisco. Working in an innovative and highly effective team environment that provides great benefits to patients, more than 180 physicians and 1,300 support personnel provide care in the 23 Sansum Clinic patient care facilities between Carpinteria and Santa Maria. The clinic has been guided by current CEO and chief medical officer Dr. Kurt Ransohoff since 1999 and provides a broad range of medical treatments. Its advanced approach has allowed its physicians to continue to lead in patient care, including performing the first carotid and laparoscopic surgeries and bringing the first digital mammography services to Santa Barbara. Yet, despite its popularity and highly regarded reputation, there are still some community-wide

misconceptions about it, according to Dr. Erno Daniel, internal medicine specialist at Sansum Clinic.

"Over the years, the word 'clinic' has come to mean different things to different people," said Daniel, who is also a leading expert on Alzheimer's disease and the clinic's historian. "Among some, there is a misconception that we are a government-sponsored clinic that deals only with the poor or indigent. That is not what we are. We are closer to being like the Mayo Clinic. We deliver the same high-quality treatment to everyone, and we are proud of our worldwide reputation for providing cutting-edge care. One-third of our patients come from other states and outside the U.S. just to be treated by our physicians."

To a large extent, the clinic has its origins in the unlikely town of Baraboo, Wisconsin, where in 1880, a 10-year-old boy, William David Sansum, declared that he wanted to be a doctor when he grew up. After graduating from Rush Medical College at the University of Chicago, Dr. Sansum began to focus on the study of insulin and the treatment of diabetes, ultimately becoming recognized as one of the leading experts in the field. In 1920, impressed by his work, the Cottage Hospital's board of trustees invited him to Santa Barbara to head the Potter Metabolic Clinic at Cottage Hospital. Sansum served there until 1932, when he opened his own clinic with 11 physicians at 317 West Pueblo Street. That site is now the parking lot for the Sansum Clinic at the same address.

Throughout his career, Sansum remained focused on refining the use of insulin for diabetes sufferers, writing numerous articles and books on the subject. Under his guidance, the first American patient ever to be injected with insulin manufactured in the United States underwent the procedure in Santa Barbara. Shortly after the operation, the *New York*

Times announced that there was a "life-saving serum" in Santa Barbara, and the newspaper report proved accurate, according to Daniel. The patient was reportedly 51 years old at the time of the operation and was diagnosed as terminally ill. After the insulin injections, he recovered and lived to be 90 years old. Sansum also pioneered work on the role of diet in diabetes and other illnesses. Until his death in 1947, Sansum was a beloved fixture in Santa Barbara. He was devoted to children suffering from diabetes and other illnesses and often took them and their families to see stage comedies on State Street.

The story of Sansum Clinic, though, is not complete without including the contributions of Dr. Rex Brown, a surgeon who founded the Santa Barbara Medical Foundation, according to Daniel. "His foundation existed alongside the Sansum Clinic for many years, but there were significant differences in how they were structured," said Daniel. "Santa Barbara was very lucky to get Dr. Brown, who counseled U.S. presidents and had a worldwide reputation. He served as a surgeon during World War I and witnessed how effective the surgical operations were in triage when all the doctors were able to consult immediately with each other. He came to Santa Barbara to found an organization that was structured with this military-style 'team orientation,' much like the Mayo Clinic had done. He also made his foundation a nonprofit. Like Dr. Sansum, he was far ahead of his time in his thinking."

Brown was also heavily involved with city planning issues and is often credited with playing a major role in

> *"Shortly after the operation, the* New York Times *announced that there was a 'life-saving serum' in Santa Barbara, and the newspaper report proved accurate."*

the reconstruction of Santa Barbara in its distinctive Mediterranean architectural style after the 1925 earthquake.

In 1998, the two clinics merged, and the best of each was forged into what is now the Sansum Clinic. The nonprofit and progressive structure of the foundation was retained, along with the visionary and advanced medical practices the original Sansum Clinic had practiced for so long.

"Doctors who love team sports love working here," said Daniel. "When you combine that with the high quality of the medicine practiced and the optimistic and positive attitude that permeates the organization, it is easy to understand why the clinic is able to attract the best doctors. Ultimately, the people we treat are the biggest beneficiaries."

A physician group board sets the standards, including personnel and procedural incomes, for the clinic. The nonprofit foundation owns and operates the buildings and grounds and makes personnel decisions. The foundation has a board of trustees made up of clinic physicians and community and business leaders. The clinic continues to play a friendly parallel role to Cottage Hospital. The two health care facilities have no formal ties, and provide competitive outpatient care, but Sansum physicians admit all their patients needing inpatient care to Cottage.

"We hope to continue what Drs. Sansum and Brown envisioned: providing comprehensive health care in all specialties," said Daniel. "People don't have to travel to Los Angeles or San Francisco to see highly skilled and caring physicians. We have them right here."

(800) 4-Sansum
www.sansumclinic.org

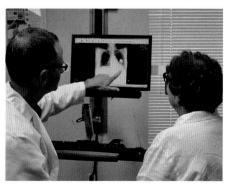

*West Coast Chiropractic
Provides Patients With a*

Holistic Approach to Healing

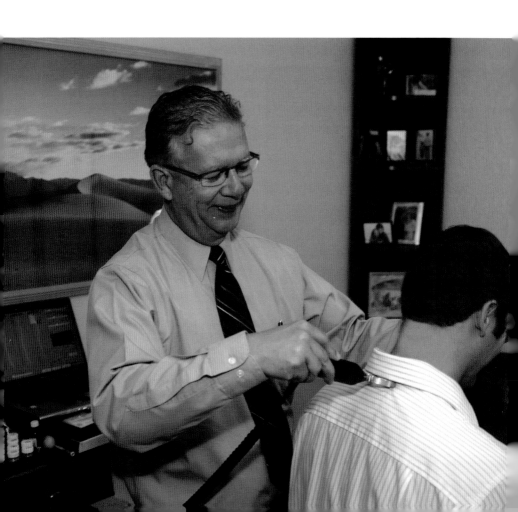

"My goal is to help as many people as I can, especially kids." With that statement Dr. Rey Alcerro, one of Santa Barbara's most experienced and respected chiropractors, expressed his personal and professional missions. Alcerro, who has had offices at 1520 State Street since 1993, focuses not only on standard chiropractic care but also on the psychological, emotional, dietary, and spiritual elements of good health.

"The pressures of modern life are huge," said Alcerro. "Stress depletes our body of nutrients and hormones and starts an entire cascade of inflammation and fatigue. I find out where the stress appears, and then we work, in a holistic way, to align and boost that part of the body. We were meant to live with joy and energy."

His wife of 21 years, Julia Alcerro, is his office manager. "Without her, I couldn't do this," he said. "She does everything that needs to be done in our lives that allows me to focus on our goals of healing as many people as we can."

Alcerro helps his patients understand the critical elements of a good diet, frame, posture, attitude, and stress-reduction processes. Alcerro has performed more than 50,000 frame adjustments and stresses that he never randomly induces motion during these adjustments but focuses on putting whatever part of the body is out of alignment back into its proper place without pain.

West Coast Chiropractic also offers food products concentrated to clinical nutritional potency. The front office is staffed by two part-time employees who offer tea, organic apples, and a welcoming attitude. Three other chiropractors and nutritionists work with Alcerro in his office complex, as part of the West Coast Holistic Wellness Center.

"My father is a great example to me," Alcerro said. "He is 94 years old and just retired from his medical practice three years ago. I see myself continuing to work here into the foreseeable future, increasing wellness in the Santa Barbara community one person at a time."

1520 State Street
Santa Barbara, CA 93101
(805) 899-2177
www.docreydc.com

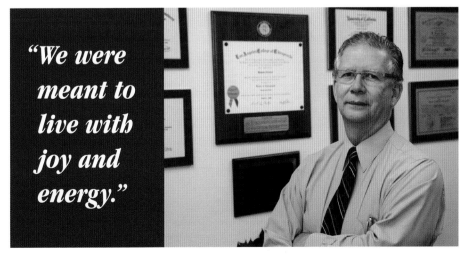

"We were meant to live with joy and energy."

Andree Clark Bird Refuge

Santa Barbara's
American Riviera Bank

If you really believe in Santa Barbara, you should bank with a local bank," said American Riviera Bank's senior vice president, Laurie Leighty, from her office at 1033 Anacapa Street. Leighty, who has been with the bank since it was founded by 405 local investors in 2006, makes a convincing argument on the community benefits of doing business locally.

"A local bank takes in deposits from the community and then lends these monies back to the businesses and other borrowers in the same community," she said. "This creates new jobs locally and improves the economy. In economic terms this is the creation of M_1 (money in circulation). Large banks take in deposits from the community, but they lend the funds wherever they can make the most money. We like to think that banking with a community bank is actually a form of creating a sustainable local economy—you deposit with a local bank, the local bank makes loans in Santa Barbara, and we all win!"

American Riviera Bank is a perfect example of that philosophy. The founders' vision—and goal—was to create a financial institution fully committed to servicing Santa Barbara. The bank, which is led by Jeff DeVine, president and CEO, and Lawrence Koppelman, chairman of the board of directors, still shapes its culture, strategies, and practices around that powerful goal.

The bank's financial footings were solid from the start. It survived the

rocky financial times in 2009 and 2010, in part because although many new banks open with less than $10 million in capital, American Riviera had an impressive $24.6 million.

American Riviera's commitment to Santa Barbara is manifested in a number of ways, including its offering of residential mortgages and construction loans at a time when many banks are moving away from

them. Decision makers, such as loan officers and senior management, are easily accessible at American Riviera. In addition, American Rivera Bank's employees volunteer in community activities, including teaching in local schools and volunteering at many local nonprofits.

In January 2013, the bank opened its second branch in the upper village of Montecito as the first tenant in the Pharmacy Development. Devine stated, "We have a considerable amount of existing clients and shareholders that live in Montecito, and they have been asking us for years when we would open a branch there. We were holding out for a very special location, and look forward to joining the other high-quality retail tenants in this center and delivering our brand of community banking to Montecito."

What is our brand of community banking? "Simply put, we are a group of experienced and knowledgeable bank professionals who are dedicated to providing customers with quick answers and solutions for their bank-ing. Combine this with the bank's state-of-the-art technology and you have a great banking experience!" said Leighty. "That's who we are."

1033 Anacapa Street
Santa Barbara, CA 93101
(805) 730-4991
www.americanrivierabank.com

"Everything We Do Is Focused on the Local Community."

ARLINGTON FINANCIAL ADVISORS, LLC

Unique Personalized Investment Strategies

Arlington Financial Advisors, LLC, is quietly separating itself from other leading investment counseling firms, so when company founders Wells Hughes, Joseph Weiland, Arthur Swalley, Dianne Duva, and John Lorenz decided in 2010 to take the bold move of starting their own firm in a town full of competitive investment companies, they knew they needed an inspired name. "We chose Arlington because it honors both the history of Santa Barbara and of the nation," said Swalley, director of investments. "That's important because half of our clients are from Santa Barbara and half from across the U.S."

Arlington investment advisors first analyze a client's financial picture and then determine goals and set strategies. The firm also has an innovative program that offers each client, from families to business owners, individualized quarterly meetings on goal setting, estate and insurance reviews, investment performance, and year-end tax planning.

The founding partners worked for Merrill Lynch until its collapse.

"Rather than join another national firm, we felt we could better serve our clients by forming our own company," said Weiland. "In large firms, you and your client have a direct relationship with the firm, but not with each other. Our clients don't have to worry whether we are offering financial packages that are best for the firm, but not necessarily for them. Our only relationship is with our clients, and our only focus is their success."

The eight-member Arlington financial team has an impressive array of degrees, certifications, registrations, and financial licenses. All have worked in the Santa Barbara area for years. "We've gotten to know our clients as people and neighbors," said Weiland, who is active in the community and is a past president of the Santa Barbara Sunrise Rotary Club. "We take care of them as family."

The company takes great pride in its community involvement. "Wealth comes in different forms, and giving back is one of the most important," said Swalley, who is vice president of the Santa Barbara Symphony. "We are dedicated to the well-being of the community."

> ## "Our only relationship is with our clients, and our only focus is their success."

100 East De La Guerra Street
Santa Barbara, CA 93101
(805) 699-7300
www.arlingtonfinancialadvisors.com

Santa Barbara's Preeminent Business Law Firm
Understands Unique Expectations of Clients

SEED MACKALL LLP

Pinpointing the key reason behind a company's success can sometimes be elusive, but in the case of Seed Mackall LLP, one of Santa Barbara's premier legal firms, it is not a difficult task.

Much like a large law firm in Los Angeles or New York, the firm offers a full range of legal services, including big firm expertise with respect to real estate and corporate matters, mergers and acquisitions, litigation, and estate planning. Seed Mackall celebrated 35 years of success in 2012, in large part because the firm understands and meets the unique expectations of its clients.

"We are working with people in Santa Barbara and elsewhere who are successful and can choose any law firm," said founding partner John Mackall (pictured at the right), whose amiable nature and extensive nonprofit work have helped create a positive community identity for the firm. "Our clients are used to the highest level of expertise, but at the same time want personalized relationships."

Largely for that reason, Mackall has stayed true to the model he estab-lished in 1977 with his founding partner, Harris Seed. The firm hires experienced attorneys who do not hand off cases to younger associates, as most large firms do.

"We consult with each other, but an attorney handles each case from the beginning to its resolution," said Mackall. "Our lawyers understand how important personal engagement and commitment are to our clients."

Of course, it doesn't hurt that the résumés of the Seed Mackall attorneys contain an all-star lineup of some of the top law schools. Mackall, for example, graduated cum laude from Harvard University and earned his law degree from Stanford University. The firm's managing partner, Tom Harding, graduated Phi Beta Kappa from Stanford and has a law degree from UC Berkeley's Boalt Hall. "The eight attorneys here all have different backgrounds and interests, which is important because we represent a broad mix of clients, from start-up tech companies and commercial real estate developers to family-owned businesses," said Harding.

Mackall, who is originally from

> "OUR LAWYERS UNDERSTAND HOW IMPORTANT PERSONAL ENGAGEMENT AND COMMITMENT ARE TO OUR CLIENTS."

Greenwich, Connecticut, said the culture and giving nature of Santa Barbara have helped shape his outlook.

"People here often don't have to be active in business anymore, but they love to give back and take on new challenges," said Mackall, who has served on a variety of nonprofit boards, including as chairman of the Cottage Health board of directors. "Clients become both friends and clients. We are inspired by the good they do. Being able to protect and advise them as legal counsel has provided great emotional payoff." It has also allowed him to enjoy 35 successful years with what one observer described as "Santa Barbara's big firm experience— without the big firm."

1332 Anacapa Street, Suite 200
Santa Barbara, CA 93101
(805) 963-0669

Goleta Valley Chamber of Commerce Advocates Innovation for Local Businesses

The Goleta Valley Chamber of Commerce, which serves 400 members representing 30,000 jobs, is celebrating its 66th anniversary. Kristen Miller, chamber president and CEO, said, "It surprises people to know that the chamber was created just after World War II and that we are a nonprofit organization. We aren't affiliated with the city, other than working with them closely to promote area businesses."

The chamber, known for its business networking breakfasts on the first Tuesday of each month, is a powerful advocate for local companies. It provides a variety of member services, including free consultations and nonpartisan political activities. The chamber publishes *Goleta Magazine* and helps members keep up with state and federal business regulations. It also communicates the views of area businesses to public officials. Members include large and small companies and single proprietors. Annual fees range from $199 to $1,300, depending on company size.

"Our biggest recent success is the Goleta Entrepreneurs Magnet (GEM) project, which involves a partnership between the chamber, UCSB, and the city of Goleta," said Miller. "We are working together to make the Goleta Valley a high-tech hot spot for entrepreneurs. It is the culmination of years of work, and we are very excited about it." The three entities are bringing together different people, different skill sets, and networking to create a mini Silicon Valley atmosphere. "GEM has the sizzle and pop that could help bring in the type of clean, high-paying industries we want," said Miller.

Full-time staff members Shelby Sim, director of business development,

and Cortney Hebert, communications coordinator, help coordinate the chamber's services, including the annual State of the City event, the Lemon Festival, and a legislative summit. The chamber was recently recognized by the Western Association of Chamber of Commerce Executives for its innovation and its leadership in "going virtual."

The GEM project will be a primary focus for the chamber in the future. "Our mission is to be a head for business and a heart for the community," said Miller. "We want to continue to create a great place for businesses and families. I am confident we can do that."

5662 Calle Real, No. 204
Goleta, CA 93117
(805) 967-2500
www.goletavalley.com

Top: Kristen Miller, president and CEO of the chamber. Bottom: During the 19th century, most of the Goleta Valley became a ranching community and a prominent lemon-growing region due to the moderate climate. The chamber puts on the Lemon Festival, celebrating Goleta's heritage, every fall.

Nonprofit Exudes Optimism in New Garden Street Headquarters

MENTAL WELLNESS CENTER

It's not often that you associate the word "optimism" with the concepts of homelessness and mental illness in Santa Barbara, but that's exactly what you'll find at the Mental Wellness Center. After a visit to the beautiful complex and a lively discussion with the center's CEO, Annmarie Cameron, you might find yourself believing there is not only hope but also answers.

The center, which last year celebrated its 65th year as a nonprofit institution in Santa Barbara, serves nearly 2,000 people annually through

its educational outreach and direct services. What motivates Cameron and the other 40 employees is the fact that treatment works. When effective treatment is provided, 80 percent of those who live with mental illnesses experience significant recovery and return to their productive role in the community. "This is a statistic that most Americans do not know," said Cameron. "The fact is mental illness is the most treatable of all the major illnesses. Once people realize this—and it is something we emphasize in our educational outreach in the schools—

the stigma currently attached to mental illness goes away. With help, the majority of the people living with symptoms of mental illness regain productive lives. That's why there is a strong sense of optimism here."

The center, which is a private charitable organization, offers a wide array of services, from affordable housing to a thriving Recovery Learning Center, the Care Closet thrift store, employment services, and an innovative Mental Health First Aid community education program. The challenge has always been how to make people

aware of these services. Cameron and other center leaders recently made two major changes that have helped increase the nonprofit's community profile.

One was the move to the new complex at 617 Garden Street, which now includes the administrative offices, the Recovery Learning Center, and 51

> ## "The fact is mental illness is the most treatable of all the major illnesses."

open, sunny apartments for persons with mental health needs and low-income downtown workers. "The affordable housing element is crucial for us because it is really challenging for anyone to effectively deal with mental illness when they are homeless," said Cameron. "It's like a family here. We celebrate everything from birthdays to when someone gets a job. People really care. Many of our employees have experienced mental illness or supported a relative with mental illness, so they can relate directly to what others are going through. They authentically offer hope and empathy."

The second change was the name change. The nonprofit had been the "Mental Health Association in Santa Barbara County" for years, but the name confused people, who thought it was part of the county system. The new name reflects the organization's action-oriented focus on overall wellness and healing. "Our new tagline is 'Recovery, Education, and Family Services,'" said Cameron.

Mental disorders strike one in four adults in the United States and cost more than $63 billion annually in lost worker productivity. Fewer than half of the children and one-third of the adults with diagnosable mental disorders receive treatment. An estimated 21 percent of local jail prisoners and 70 percent of youth in the juvenile justice system have at least one mental health disorder.

The Mental Wellness Center operates a licensed board and care home, Casa Juana Maria, which offers 24-hour care for six adults; runs the Eleanor Apartments, which provide independent living for 16 adults; and provides many other forms of residential support. A key feature at the facility is the Recovery and Learning Center, which includes a large, white, gleaming, plaza-like area where people can sit and have a meal, visit, and enjoy the day in a safe environment. "It's a clean,

supportive space where people can come to become engaged in mental wellness and recovery," said Cameron.

The nonprofit offers a host of other critically important services. "When you have a mental illness it affects the entire family," said Cameron. "Many times parents find us after their son or daughter is diagnosed either in jail or in a psychiatric hospital. The parents often aren't ready for the diagnosis, and they are frightened and bewildered."

Those using the center's services learn how to deal with mental illness and how to navigate the sometimes complicated and frustrating governmental health systems. "Ironically, a lot of our best volunteers are parents who became frustrated over what they see as a 'broken' governmental system, and now they want to help others," said Cameron. The Mental Wellness Center provides a programmatic home to the National Alliance on Mental Illness, and together they offer Family to Family classes twice a year.

Perhaps the biggest community challenge remains the stigma of mental illness. To help combat this, the center has embarked on an aggressive community educational program called "Mental Health Matters." "We educate about 400 sixth-grade students in Santa Barbara annually," said Camer-on. "We teach them that mental illness is nothing to be ashamed of and that it is treatable. The students are curious and receptive. I am very proud of how this program has been received."

The center has also offered job-finding services since 2010. More than 200 people have been helped with support in retraining and job placements so far.

This year the center will again offer the innovative Mental Health First Aid program, which equips people with skills to handle a mental health crisis they might encounter in their home or in public. Much like a first-aid class, this prepares people to help others who are experiencing symptoms of mental illness and provides them with pragmatic steps to support someone until professional help is provided.

"We have a seven-year plan that includes some bold initiatives to secure endowment funds for specific services," said Cameron. "We want to be assured of long-term sustainability. So far, the community has responded in a very supportive way. Santa Barbara stands beside us. With this continued support, we can help make great strides."

617 Garden Street
Santa Barbara, CA 93101
(805) 884-8440
www.mentalwellnesscenter.org

Rotary International Is Dedicated to
Humanitarian Service

Rotary International, a volunteer organization of business and professional leaders who provide humanitarian service and promote goodwill and peace worldwide, has some 1.2 million members in more than 200 countries. Founded in Chicago in 1905, the Rotary Foundation has awarded about $2.1 billion in grants worldwide, which are administered at the community level by Rotary clubs.

In 1985, Rotary International created PolioPlus—a program to immunize the world's children against polio. To date, Rotary has contributed at least $1 billion and countless volunteer hours to the vaccination of more than 2 billion children in 122 countries. These efforts have been credited with the near global eradication of the disease. Rotarians intend to see the polio eradication project through to the finish. The vaccine supply chains and vaccination methods pioneered by Rotary and their partners will make it easier to eradicate other diseases plaguing vulnerable populations around the world.

The Rotary motto is "Service Above Self," and the 375 members of the eight local Rotary clubs live out that mission through fundraisers, activities, and services that benefit schools, playgrounds, parks, and other neighborhood resources. Two Rotary clubs sponsor the 4th of July fireworks at Goleta's Girsh Park; the Carpinteria Morning Club helped build and furnish equipment for the Tomol Playground; and all the clubs work with local schools, including providing dictionaries for area third graders.

Friendly cooperation and fun are at the heart of the Rotary experience, and Rotarians enjoy community service in an atmosphere of relaxed fellowship. Most Rotarians join the club at the invitation of other Rotarians, but new members come from all economic and cultural backgrounds. For more information, contact any of the local clubs, or learn about Rotary International at www.rotary.org.

Below: Rotarians decorating a float for the rose parade.

ROTARY CLUB OF CARPINTERIA MORNING

Meets: Wednesdays at 7:00 a.m.
Woman's Club
1071 Vallecito Road
www.carpmorningrotary.org/

ROTARY CLUB OF CARPINTERIA

Meets: Thursdays at 11:45 a.m.
Lion's Community Park
6197 Casitas Pass Road
www.carpinteriarotary.org

ROTARY CLUB OF GOLETA NOONTIME

Meets: Tuesdays at 11:45 a.m.
Elephant Bar Restaurant
521 Firestone Road
www.goletanoontimerotary.org

ROTARY CLUB OF GOLETA

Meets: 2nd and 4th Tuesdays
at 6:30 p.m.
Elephant Bar Restaurant
www.rotaryclubofgoleta.org

ROTARY CLUB OF MONTECITO

Meets: Tuesdays at 12:10 p.m.
Montecito Country Club
920 Summit Road
www.montecitorotary.org

ROTARY CLUB OF SANTA BARBARA

Meets: Fridays at 12:00 p.m.
Fess Parker's Doubletree Resort
633 East Cabrillo Road
www.clubrunner.ca/Portal/Home.
aspx?cid=2852

ROTARY CLUB OF SANTA BARBARA SUNRISE

Meets: Wednesdays at 7:00 a.m.
Santa Barbara Club
1105 Chapala Street
www.sbsunriserotary.org

ROTARY CLUB OF SANTA BARBARA NORTH

Meet: Wednesdays at 12:00 p.m.
Harry's Plaza Café
3313 State Street
www.rotaryclubsbnorth.org

In October 2012, a fire broke out in the rugged high country above Goleta and a firefighter fell on a steep slope, injuring his leg. The Santa Barbara County Search and Rescue (SAR) team, a volunteer branch of the Santa Barbara County Sheriff's Department, had just finished delivering evacuation notices to the residents of Painted Cave. The team was called and raced through the smoke-filled canyons and hills to reach him. The injured firefighter was placed in a stretcher, and the SAR team fought through thick brush and steep, rocky terrain to bring him to safety as aircraft dropped fire retardant on the fire above them. "It took incredible teamwork to climb the canyons, lower him down the waterfalls, and get him to safety," said Valerie Walston, SAR public information officer, who also took part in the rescue. "But it is what we train for and what we do. We're not happy unless we're going on a call."

Stories of the heroics of the Santa Barbara County SAR team make headlines on occasion, but most of the community remains unaware that the 38 members of the Santa Barbara County group are unpaid volunteers. The organization is a nonprofit and does not charge for rescues.

Although the team is called out on an average of 140 emergencies every year, the team must rely on annual fundraising efforts for at least part of its budget.

Santa Barbara County Search and Rescue Team Volunteers with Heart and Courage

"The county does pick up part of the expense, but the administration, recruitment, and training programs are operated by the team itself, a nonprofit, public benefit corporation," explained Jim Frank, SAR incident commander. "Although when we respond on a call or are training, we are a volunteer unit of the Santa Barbara County Sheriff's Department." The rescue team is made up of a cross section of the community, including

business owners, hospital workers, engineers, a geologist, computer programmers, accountants, and a "couple of PhDs," according to Frank.

The SAR organization celebrated its 50th anniversary in 2012. Each volunteer is dedicated to a high level of training and professionalism that was set long ago. "It is a wonderful outdoor community here, but things happen in the outdoors," said Frank. "We're one of 100 member teams of the Mountain Rescue Association, and as they say, the mountains don't care whether you make it back or not, but we do. We will be there to help you if something goes wrong."

The SAR team, which is often the busiest rescue team in California, provides a variety of services. The Dick Smith and San Rafael Wilderness areas, along with the rugged expanses of the Los Padres National Forest, are some of the most isolated wild lands in California. Rescues there can be complicated and often require intricate teamwork and careful planning. Along with searching for lost hikers, the team is trained and equipped to perform swift-water rescues, locate downed aircraft and respond to wilderness area vehicle and hiking accidents. Most of the volunteers are certified emergency medical technicians, are trained for helicopter deployment into the wilderness, and have mastered high-angle rescue techniques, such as rope rappels.

"I can't stress enough what an exceptional group of people this is,"

"The mountains don't care whether you make it back or not, but we do."

said Frank. "We take this job very seriously, but we also have a lot of fun in the training." The SAR team is equipped with an impressive fleet of 16 rescue vehicles, including an ex-military Humvee, several four-wheel-drive trucks, quads, and Suburbans. A search dog certified through the California Rescue Dog Association is also a valuable member of the team.

The Santa Barbara County Sheriff's Department operates the Project Lifesaver program locally. This program helps persons with Alzheimer's disease, dementia, or mental dysfunction disorders, and youngsters with Down syndrome or autism, who tend to wander. The SAR team provides the "search" function of this program and supports the Sheriff's Department in searches for other "at risk" adults and children.

In the 50 years the SAR team has been serving Santa Barbara County, more than 2,000 people have received their help. Many of the distress calls come from hikers who have become lost or dehydrated. "One of the things we highly recommend to hikers is to make certain they bring an adequate supply of water with them," said Frank. "People often don't realize the temperatures can get very hot and dry in the mountains, even on the popular front country trails."

Many of the rescues have been dramatic, often with lives on the line. Twenty or so years ago, two

lost UCSB students were rescued near Lizard's Mouth after they took a wrong turn on a trail. It was dark, windy, and snowing when SAR members found the students, who were wearing only T-shirts and shorts, and saved their lives with a portable hot-air tank and space blankets. The SAR team was active during the Montecito Tea, Jesusita, and Goleta Gap fires in 2008 and 2009, and they train regularly for urban rescues in case of a disaster like an earthquake or a major mudslide.

As a public-benefit, nonprofit organization, the SAR relies on strong community support. The Wood-Claeyssens, Santa Barbara, Hutton Parker, Orfalea, and Raintree founda-tions have all been major supporters, according to Walston.

"Our rescue team is made up of people in the community who want to help," said Frank. "Imagine yourself in the back country, injured and all alone in the rain and the darkness. We are the ones who are going to come and get you. We are trained to do that. We aren't paid to do it, but there is a real sense of satisfaction in doing something few others can do. Bringing people home safely is reward enough for us."

(805) 967-0253
www.sbcsar.net

St. Vincent's

Creating Hope for Low-Income Families Since 1858

In the winter of 1858, the Daughters of Charity of St. Vincent de Paul first arrived in Santa Barbara by steamer from the East Coast, stepping onto the beach where Stearns Wharf is today. They had a mission in mind—to help the underserved children of the community get the care and education they needed.

Today, St. Vincent's, the oldest existing charitable organization in Santa Barbara, is still true to that mission. In its beautiful complex off Calle Real near the Highway 154 exit, the organization continues to educate, house, and care for hundreds of children and their families. St. Vincent's also offers affordable housing for seniors. The story of the longevity, success, and unwavering vision of the sisters at St. Vincent's remains one of the most amazing and relatively unknown stories in Santa Barbara. For years, the organization was visible to the community because of the large signature building that could be seen from the roadway, but the structure was demolished a few years ago, and

the public's awareness of St. Vincent's seemed to diminish.

When Sister Margaret Keaveney, D.C., came to Santa Barbara from the San Jose area to direct St. Vincent's in 2010, she vowed to remind the community that the organization was alive and well. "We want Santa Barbara to know that we are still here and providing all the help we can to those mothers and their children who might be struggling," she said. "We've been here since the beginning, and we will be here in the years to come. We are very excited about what is happening at St. Vincent's, and we want to share it with everyone."

St. Vincent's Family Strengthening Program provides a safe haven for single mothers and their children that includes affordable housing, help in finding jobs, a food and clothing pantry, early schooling and special tutoring for children ages one to five years, addiction counseling, family

Opposite: The Daughters of Charity of St. Vincent de Paul at the St. Vincent's Administration Building, December 2011

"We help them to find their personal dignity—that place within them—that says they are worthy, that their hopes and dreams are attainable, and that they are able to play a positive role in their children's lives."

interventions, and special offerings such as a community garden. The mothers and their children live in the housing units for up to two years, while they strengthen themselves, bond with their children, and prepare for the future.

"The mothers who come here seeking our help are noble women," said Keaveney. "They were rarely affirmed in their lives, often domestically battered, and some are victims of addiction. We help them to find their personal dignity—that place within them—that says they are worthy, that their hopes and dreams are attainable, and that they are able to play a positive role in their children's lives. It is amazing to see how these women grow when they are given a safe place to live, support for the attainment of their hopes, and help for their children. It's a wonderful thing to watch them turn their lives around and become good, devoted mothers and productive members of the community."

The modern, Spanish-style housing offered to the families is critical to the women's ability to feel comfortable and secure, often for the first time in their lives. In addition to the housing for mothers and children in St. Vincent's Family Strengthening Program, there are 75 two- and three-bedroom units for low-income families at St. Vincent's Gardens and 95 units for low-income seniors at Villa Caridad. The well-landscaped environment

Left, top to bottom: Sister Mary Ann Tippett, D.C., and a child in the After School Program, April 2012. St. Vincent's Community Garden, where wisdom and youth meet, April 2012. The children at St. Vincent's Early Childhood Education Center, April 2012. (Photos by Larry Hirshowitz)

also includes a swimming pool and basketball court for residents to use. The waiting list for the Affordable Housing Programs is nearly five years, according to Keaveney. "That shows how many families out there are in need of our services," she said.

The licensed Catholic Early Childhood Education Center provides quality, affordable child care for infants six weeks old to children five years old. It includes a preschool and educational opportunities to help prepare children for their entrance into kindergarten.

St. Vincent's Heart has an on-site volunteer-assisted food pantry and donation center. Fresh food is distributed weekly to the families, along with clothing, shoes, baby goods, school supplies, books, toys, and other household necessities. "It is a very popular program," said Keaveney. "We encourage community donations of things like sheets, cribs, blankets, pots, pans, and dishes. Each family takes those with them when they leave us, so we are in constant need of them. Children's clothing, especially things like jackets for winter, is very welcome. We encourage those who want to donate to call us before coming in, so we can be there to make sure everything goes smoothly."

Many of the women and children in St. Vincent's Family Strengthening Program build friendships and help each other. They share the same hopes and aspirations for their families, and they learn from each other's experiences, as well as from the licensed counselors and teachers who are available.

"I asked one young woman if she was going home for Thanksgiving with her child, and she shook her head 'no,'" said Keaveney. "The woman was about 20 years old. She said, 'My parents are on drugs, and I don't want my child around them.' That's the pattern of living we are trying to help them break. She stayed here and had a happy Thanksgiving. Many of the women go on to do impressive things. One is now an engineering student at UCSB. It's great to see them succeed after they have suffered such hardships."

The heritage of St. Vincent's runs deep. Within a week of the sisters' arrival in Santa Barbara in 1858, they established the first English-speaking school and orphanage in the region. They opened the first hospital infirmary 15 years later and the first orphanage and school for developmentally disabled children in 1936. During this long stretch of history, as Santa Barbara grew, St. Vincent's was always there, providing support, education, and shelter. "We are so grateful to the benefactors, supporters, volunteers, and staff who have journeyed with us over the years," said Keaveney.

"It is a place of safety, hope, and healing," said Keaveney. "We are all united on this earth and in this place. For the women here, the commonality is the hope that all parents have for their children. Our goals for the future are the same as they have been in the past: to help make those hopes come true."

4200 Calle Real
Santa Barbara, CA 93110
(805) 683-6381
www.stvincents-sb.org

youth interactive

Innovative Nonprofit for At-Risk Students Teaches Technology and Entrepreneurship

he founding of the innovative and exciting nonprofit Youth Interactive has an intriguing international aspect. At first glance, it seems similar to other youth programs. Its mission statement, "To help transform Santa Barbara's at-risk youth from potential dropout statistics to college-bound high school graduates," is familiar. But after one conversation with its charismatic founder and president, Nathalie Gensac, it becomes clear that this is a cutting-edge and visionary effort with global connections.

While visiting major cities on several continents as the host of a television travel show, Gensac, who was born in Versailles, France, and educated in England, was deeply moved by the vast number of poverty-stricken children she encountered. In 2005, she quit her television job and embarked on a different kind of world journey, one focused on combating the suffering she witnessed. Using her considerable persuasive skills, she gained backing and established programs in India, Jamaica, and parts of the United States. Youth Interactive now serves more than 2,000 youth worldwide and is looking to expand to Papua, New Guinea. When she was looking for a home base, Gensac focused on Santa Barbara for many reasons, including its strong charitable nature and the growing need for such a program in the city.

She spent two years talking to school, government, and charity leaders and parents to determine how to best serve children in need in the city. What emerged was a new model, one that directly connects with today's youth. Although helping at-risk young people is not a new concept, the magic of Youth Interactive is in the how.

"We are connecting with these kids in their own language and on their own terms," said Gensac. "By that I mean what we call TEA, which is technology, entrepreneurship, and the arts. We are employing 3D technology and the arts to help them find their passion and build self-confidence. We also provide them with a vehicle to develop their own businesses and acquire entrepreneurial skills. Youth Interactive is not a teen center; it is far

more. We teach students how to help themselves."

The kids are encouraged and taught how to create different art products, such as building outdoor furniture with wine barrel staves, which are sold at the center and other places. The youth keep a percentage of their profits. This is a critical element of the model because of the economic sustainability aspect, according to Gensac. It allows the youth to not only directly connect their artistic efforts to income and entrepreneurship but it also provides an ongoing source of funds for the center that can be reinvested into future projects.

Youth Interactive serves up to 35 young people a day at its colorful and cheerful lower Anacapa Street headquarters. These young people are linked via the Internet to youth in Jamaica and India and often trade ideas. The center offers a computer bar for the young people and substantive

multimedia equipment and instructions offered by partner organizations such as Cage Free Productions. Also included are programs in 3D formats where students can learn production and other skills. These formats can be highly beneficial to kids with learning disabilities and ADHD. The center also provides one-on-one tutoring and group study sessions after school.

Gensac, who was nominated for an Ernst & Young Social Entrepreneur of the Year Award for her work, has also formed strong relationships with many other Santa Barbara nonprofits, which are lending great support to Youth Interactive. Among them are EasyLift, which provides safe transportation to youth who can't afford to travel to the facility. The service is often used for youth coming from gang areas and the housing authority. Palabra, founded by community activist Juan Pablo Herrada, which serves kids mostly in the Latino community, and Willow Rock Writers, whose volunteers teach English skills, have also teamed with Youth Interactive. Marcia Meier, well known as the former director of the Santa Barbara Writer's Conference, is overseeing the center's writing program.

Another key supporter of Youth Interactive is the Food Bank, which provides the center with healthy organic food every afternoon. This is critical because participants often do not get a balanced meal at home. Youth Interactive is sponsored by a variety of other community organizations and individuals, including Montecito Bank and Trust, the J.S. Bower Foundation, the Santa Barbara Foundation, the Santa Barbara Arts Commission, the McCune Foundation, the Fund for Santa Barbara, Citrix, and Lynda.com.

Gensac's commitment to charitable and nonprofit causes makes her a perfect fit in Santa Barbara, home of some of the most altruistic people on

"The kids light up when they begin to trust they are going to be supported."

earth. Her motivation stems from her own difficult childhood in France, where she was essentially abandoned as a young teenager on the streets of Paris. A few caring adults made a critical difference in her life, and Gensac vowed to do the same for others. She has not drawn a salary for years but insists that the emotional payoff has been substantial. "I am permanently intellectually stimulated by this," she said. "But emotionally, the rewards are even greater. The kids light up when they begin to trust they are going to be supported. They become positive and productive and dare to become themselves," she said. "It's a beautiful thing to see."

209 Anacapa Street
Santa Barbara, CA 93101
(805) 453-4123

East Beach

Santa Barbara Airbus Offers Friendly Reliable Service to
LAX and Beyond

Sometimes a company takes on the best qualities of its owners and thrives because of it. Once you get to know the founders of the Santa Barbara Airbus, Eric Onnen (pictured below on the right), his wife Kelly, and their partner Mark Klopstein (pictured below on the left), it quickly becomes apparent that this is such a company. Known primarily for its reliable and comfortable bus transportation to and from the Los Angeles International Airport (LAX), "The Airbus," as it is known, was established in 1983.

Today, its 25-bus fleet travels more than 1.2 million miles annually and is one of Santa Barbara's most successful enterprises.

Located in a new facility at 750 Technology Drive in Goleta, the Airbus offers eight round-trips per day, 363 days per year. Passengers can board at the company headquarters (where they can park long term for $30), at the Hyatt Hotel in Santa Barbara, and in Carpenteria. From there it is nonstop to the LAX terminal of their choice.

"The LAX ground transportation is what we are most known for, but we also offer charter trips and specialty day trips and tours," said Eric. The drivers are friendly, the buses are immaculately clean, and the entire 60-employee staff seems upbeat, reflecting the attitude of the owners. The company recently won the Pacific Coast Business Times and the U.S. Small Business Administration joint award for exemplary practices in a family-owned business. It also won the California Bus Association's Outstanding Operator of the Year for 2012. The company is certified as a green business by the county because of its strong environmental awareness.

"We are a transportation company, but we really are a customer service company," said Eric. "We never forget that." Exemplifying its commitment is the innovative reservation system Eric pioneered early in the company's history, which is now handled on the phone or Internet. Airbus was one of the first bus operators to take reservations, and the system is known for being easy to use, even for first-timers.

The demand for the charter aspect of the business and the culturally oriented trips continues to grow every year. Last year the company sold out several trips to a variety of concerts and plays, along with a trip to Albuquerque, New Mexico.

The Airbus was founded after Eric and Kelly, who was then a Canadian flight attendant, were married 31 years ago. During their courtship, Eric had to make multiple round trips by car from Santa Barbara to LAX to accommodate Kelly's flight schedule. It was Kelly's father who suggested that Santa Barbara needed a commuter bus line to the airport. Eric, a business major at UCSB, was intrigued by the idea, and the Airbus was born. Since then the company, based on convenience, reliability, and customer service, has prospered.

750 Technology Drive
Santa Barbara, CA 93117
(805) 964-7759

> **"We are a transportation company, but we really are a customer service company."**

Santa Barbara's HR Department on Demand

People shouldn't have to hate going to work." With that simple sentence, Kerry McCoy, president and co-founder of HRxpress, Santa Barbara's only "Human Resource Department on Demand," revealed not only her powerful corporate mission but also her positive view of life.

HRxpress, created in 1997 by McCoy (pictured below on the right) and Santa Barbara colleagues Beverly Wood (on the left) and Alice Bourland, provides small and midsize companies with a full array of human resource (HR) functions, from consulting and organizational development to governmental compliance and HR administration. The company uses a Web-based system and employs only senior HR experts, including Helene Schneider, who also currently serves as the mayor of Santa Barbara. As an outsource HR agency, the company fills a unique niche that area executives are often thrilled to discover.

"We hear, 'Oh, I love you! I'm so glad you exist!' quite a bit," said McCoy, with a smile. "People in new or smaller businesses often undervalue the HR element, and they find them-

selves retroactively trying to organize it out of chaos when they grow. It's satisfying and a lot of fun for us to be there to help them."

HRxpress was created when McCoy, Wood, and Bourland decided to combine their extensive HR experience. "We said, 'Why don't we start a business?'" said McCoy. "Then suddenly we had to get serious when, to our surprise, we got a contract with the city of Buellton to write their job descriptions." McCoy and Wood are still co-owners of the business after 15 years.

Driving it all, though, is a deep sense of mission and purpose. More than just satisfying companies' HR needs, HRxpress is committed to helping build positive, productive work cultures. "We can write an employee handbook for you," said McCoy, "but we can also help you evaluate and create a healthy environment where people will produce their best work. We get the most gratification in helping you build a joyous, exciting, and enthusiastic company. It's easier than it looks."

One thing that isn't easy for many companies is complying with California's complex employee labor laws, which McCoy said are among the most difficult and "expensively dangerous" in the country. Many executives are relieved to leave the difficult task of compliance to HRxpress.

The company, located at 219 West Carrillo Street in Santa Barbara, has dozens of clients. It is especially active with nonprofit organizations. "We have a soft spot for our local nonprofits," said McCoy. "We love working with them because they're working for us."

Asked about the future, McCoy said she and Wood are thinking of palm trees and umbrella drinks. "We're hoping that just the right entrepreneur will come along and take what is a great business opportunity to the next level."

219-A West Carrillo Street
Santa Barbara, CA 93101
(805) 965-7733

Premier Photographer and Teacher Finds Success Through Diversity and Reasonable Prices

Three words define Scott Gibson's photography: quality, diversity, and fun. Over his 22-year professional career, Scott has photographed more than 600 weddings; has worked with the region's top real estate agents, advertising/PR firms, corporations, and organizations; and has contributed cover photos to major newspapers and magazines. His photos grace the pages and front cover of *Community Builders.*

By offering a wide range of photography products and services at reasonable prices, he is experiencing his greatest business success, in spite of the bad economy and increased competition. Gibson also owns and operates the largest postcard and souvenir publishing and distributing company in Santa Barbara. In addition, he has developed excellent Photoshop skills, which are essential in today's photography industry.

Gibson stands behind his work 100 percent. "If someone asks my guarantee policy, I tell them they don't owe me a nickel if they don't love their photos," he said. "I also think it is very important how the whole process of a photography job happens. I like to say, 'There's no reason this can't be a little bit of fun.'"

Weddings are a special focus for Gibson, who has photographed them since graduating from Westmont College in 1988. Although anyone can snap a photo, Gibson says success in wedding photography still takes hard work, experience, and talent.

This year Gibson plans to increase his focus on workshops and speaking engagements about the business of photography, something he sees as his future. He targets amateur photographers who want to improve or become professionals and pros who want to increase their skill set and job opportunities. "As the population of photographers increases, I see an almost unlimited demand for photography knowledge of all types," he said. "There is an entire generation of new, struggling photographers trying to charge top dollar in one area of photography, and only working a few days a month. I see a tremendous opportunity to teach them how to diversify their skill set and treat their photography business like a full-time job instead of a get-rich-quick scheme." He adds, "It's very satisfying to help others benefit from what I have learned over the years."

(805) 570-0692
www.gibsonpix.com

"He cares deeply about his clients' satisfaction."

— Jeff Boehm, publisher of *Santa Barbara Community Builders,* on Scott Gibson

A Santa Barbara Sunset

Santa Barbara
POLO & RACQUET CLUB
Is Affordable, Fun, and Open to Everyone

The 102-year-old Santa Barbara Polo & Racquet Club showcases some of the best polo played in the world. Polo players traverse the globe year-round in search of great weather conditions and perfect turf, and the club is famous for consistently providing both. The polo season runs from May through October, and the 1 p.m. and 3 p.m. Sunday matches are open to the public. At only $10 per person for most Sunday matches, tickets are a great sports and social entertainment value. If you haven't seen a match, you will want to come feel the thrill of it firsthand. Watching the joint athleticism of the players and their horses while they navigate between the goals at 20+ miles per hour is riveting, plus spectators get the enjoyment of stomping the divots at half time, a la the movie *Pretty Woman*. So don your largest hat and step back in time to a more gracious era.

Founded in 1911 and steeped in history, the 500-member Polo & Racquet Club remains a self-sustaining nonprofit organization. The fields act as a stunning backdrop for upscale special events, such as car shows, music festivals, weddings, and a variety of fundraising efforts, such as the Avon Breast Cancer Walk, the annual Women of

the Braille Institute Auxiliary gala, and several charity exhibition polo matches. Buck Brannaman, the gentleman cowboy and famed "horse whisperer" portrayed by Robert Redford in the recent biography of his life, visited the club in April. The event drew a large crowd that enjoyed watching him conduct a multiple-day horsemanship workshop in a full-size show-quality arena.

The unique facility includes a set of grandstands with upper box seating available, a fine dining restaurant that serves brunch, a café and full bar, along with private cabanas that can be rented. Tailgating spots are available too if you prefer to sit under an umbrella or spread a blanket on the thick, lush grass. Stables for 350 horses and 87 acres of landscaped polo fields are part of the ambience. Fulfilling the "& Racquet Club" part of the organization, the site has eight tennis courts adjacent to Foothill Road as well as swimming and fitness clubs. "This is a very friendly place," says Ariana Nobel, general manager. "Our tennis, swim-

ming and fitness clubs are as affordable as any in the entire Santa Barbara region, and we pride ourselves on our family-friendly atmosphere."

The tennis club lies tucked between the polo fields and the dramatic rise of the Carpinteria foothills behind. The sunsets are extraordinary because the ocean view can be seen from the upper grounds. The facilities boast newly renovated locker rooms, Jacuzzis, six well-lighted courts, and one jovial tennis director, Bart Hillock, who has overseen the club for 20 years and retains his youthful energy and easy smile. The level of tennis played here varies from beginners in the junior leagues and camps to very high. In fact, one of the pros, Stephanie Baker Stone, is headed to Turkey to represent the USA team at the world championships of senior women's tennis in November 2013. Youth lessons for polo, tennis, and swimming (the pool is kept at 85 degrees year round) are available, and a two-week polo training camp for youth is held each July. At the camp, students live on-site

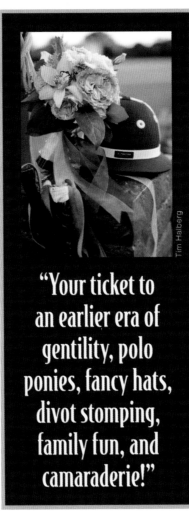

Tim Halberg

"Your ticket to an earlier era of gentility, polo ponies, fancy hats, divot stomping, family fun, and camaraderie!"

and learn horsemanship from top-ranked players from around the globe. Hour and a half long polo training classes for high school, collegiate, and adult players cost $100 and include the mount and all equipment.

The Sunday polo matches bring top teams from around the world and are fast, athletic, and intensely entertaining. "Even for the most seasoned residents of Santa Barbara, who have seen it all, this is something different, exciting, and very special," said Alison Hansen, event and sales director. "We pride ourselves on giving all of our guests the VIP treatment along with a historical and cultural experience."

3300 Via Real
Carpinteria, CA 93013
(805) 684-6683
www.sbpolo.com

Photos by Tim Halberg

CITRIX

Goleta's Global Tech Leader Floats on a 'Cloud' of Success

Citrix is a quintessential modern success story, complete with a garage-to-global tale of technological innovation and inspired management. The company's Online Services division was formed in 2004, when Citrix purchased Expertcity, a local start-up begun in 1997 as the brainchild of a professor and two graduate students from UCSB. Today, the company provides remote connectivity and online collaboration solutions to customers worldwide. The Online Services division employs more than 1,500 of the 8,000+ Citrix employees globally, including more than 600 people at its Goleta campus, making it one of the largest private employers in Santa Barbara County.

"People in Santa Barbara know we have grown quickly, but I'm not sure they know just how fast we are expanding," said Brett Caine, senior vice president and general manager of the Citrix Online Services division. "It's been satisfying and a lot of fun to be a part of this type of growth."

The company provides cloud-based solutions that enable mobile workstyles—letting people work from anywhere, with anyone, and on any device. Its offerings include GoToMyPC, GoToMeeting, GoToWebinar, GoToTraining, GoToAssist, Podio, and ShareFile. Citrix is currently the second-largest web-conferencing provider in the world, according to Caine.

Technological savvy isn't the only reason for the company's amazing success. It also attracts talented personnel because of its employee-centric mission and values. "We've tried hard to make this a great place to work, and I think it says a lot that two of the cofounders are still here," said Caine. "Bernd Christiansen is our chief technology officer, and Malte Muenke is our VP of engineering and customer operations. We also have many other employees who have been with us for more than 10 years. It is this focus on employees which enables us to deliver on our growth and profit goals—growing our business from $40M at acquisition to more than 10 times that in 2011."

Caine has helmed the Online Services division for the past nine years. During that time, Citrix has become increasingly involved with giving back to the Santa Barbara region, embody-ing their "work better, live better" motto. "We support our employees' interests in the community by matching employee contributions to qualifying nonprofits and offering 16 paid hours of volunteer time every year." The company also partners with over 75 local nonprofits and donated more than $2.5 million in products to charities worldwide in 2012. "It's a big part of who we are," said Caine.

www.citrixonline.com

Innovation Drives
COASTAL COPY
to the Top

"Our strength is our service, but we also pay a great deal of attention to getting the best technology available."

A framed, handwritten ledger full of names and numbers hangs on the wall of the Coastal Copy Company to remind owner Tom Rizk of its origins. "The ledger was written in the late 1970s by the former owner in an effort to get me to buy the company," said Rizk. "As you can see, the profit in those days was counted in the hundreds of dollars."

Under Rizk's leadership, the office equipment sales and service company now has 32 employees and is one of the largest companies of its kind in the three-county area. The business-to-business company provides printing, copying, and scanning solutions and services for more than 20,000 copy machines for such clients as Cottage Hospital and the San Luis Obispo and Santa Barbara school districts.

"We work primarily in eight vertical markets—government, health care, law, faith-based organizations, schools, insurance, manufacturing, and car dealerships," said Rizk. "A lot of people look at our name and think we're like Kinko's, where they can come and have copies made. While we are happy to do that, we are a different kind of company."

Rizk credits part of his success to Coastal Copy's unique service program. "We make house calls," he said. "I have five technicians who make about 3,000 inspections per month, making sure our clients have the supplies they need and their machines are working. It's all about service. People want to push the button and have the copies come out."

Rizk says the company's service manager, Tony Przybyla, has helped the company stay ahead of the curve technologically. "Our strength is our service, but we pay a great deal of effort to getting the best technology available," Rizk said.

Giving back to the community is also important, and the company has donated nearly 1,000 copy machines to charitable organizations. In addition, Rizk has served on dozens of nonprofit boards and continues to support the Carpinteria Boys' Club. "Our ability to give back is a big part of the satisfaction of building this business," he said.

(800) 995-8835
www.coastalcopy.com

Deckers Outdoor Corporation

Perhaps no company in America has more "soul" than Deckers, an upstart turned global culture leader that is discreetly headquartered near the Santa Barbara Airport in Goleta. Of course, you could also spell that "sole" and still be correct. Deckers was launched in 1973 by college student Doug Otto, who created a brand of crazy, multilayered flip-flops that caught the imagination of the then long-haired baby boomers. Staying focused primarily on outdoor, athletic, fashion-oriented, and casual footwear, the company has thrived. This year marks the 40th anniversary of Deckers, and its global footprint is greater than ever. Today, Deckers owns the world-famous UGG® Australia brand, the popular outdoor adventure brand Teva®, the rising surf-inspired Sanuk® brand, and four smaller brands it is incubating with resources and expertise.

"We are a global company," said Angel Martinez, president, CEO, and chairman of the board of directors. "We have offices throughout Asia, Europe, the UK, and the U.S. It creates for us a broad worldview, allowing us to bring talented people to Santa Barbara from many different countries."

The company's corporate success story is nothing short of remarkable. Since Martinez took the helm in 2005, the publically held company's revenues have skyrocketed from $200 million to $1.3 billion in 2011.

The company's success can be credited to a winning combination of innovative product design, an exemplary company culture, and strong leadership. The growth of the company led Martinez, one of the most respected CEOs in the country, to secure a new site for the company's Goleta headquarters. The new facility, which will house more than 400 employees, will be located at the Cabrillo Business Park in Goleta. It will include a 20-acre campus with LEED (Leadership in Energy and En-

ONE VISION · MANY TEAMS · ONE FAMILY

vironmental Design) certified buildings, improved city streets, reclaimed wetlands landscaping, bike paths, and public transportation infrastructure. It will also house an impressive retail showcase. This is a key part of Deckers's efforts to become an even more integral part of the Santa Barbara community. "We will have a store where all of our brands are displayed and that will likely become a destination," said Martinez. "Visitors will be able to see that we have a vibrant enterprise here. We hope to improve a corner of the community and stimulate entrepreneurial activity in the area with the creation of our new corporate headquarters."

The physical improvements, though, are only one way the company has sought to become a premier corporate citizen of Santa Barbara. Not only does Deckers have a significant effect on the local economy, with more than 400 employees, but it has also become a model for positive corporate culture. The classic elements of fostered teamwork, employee recognition, shared vision, and common goals are all embedded there. Martinez and the human resources team aggressively recruit for world-class talent. "We are very picky about who we allow into the company," said Martinez. "We look for skills and experience, but most of all we are looking to see what kind of character the person has. We support each other here, and that's a major element of any job interview—getting to the core of a person's character."

Martinez developed his leadership values as one of the first three employees at Reebok. He learned about teamwork even earlier. "I ran

on a cross-country team when I was younger, and I learned quickly that a team is only as fast as its slowest runner," he said. "However, I also learned you can do amazing things when you all work together, and what it is about a team that allows for maximum performance. We do all those things here, and our employees respond to it. I am proud of the fact that Deckers is different." The company has been singled out for its progressive culture. For example, *Outside* magazine has included Deckers on its annual list of "Best Places to Work" four times in the five years that the magazine has published the list.

The company is actively involved with the Santa Barbara community, and its employees have spent thousands of hours volunteering their time for charitable causes. "We offer up to 24 hours of paid time for employees who use that time to work for

> "We hope to improve a corner of the community and **stimulate entrepreneurial activity** in the area with the creation of our new corporate headquarters."

nonprofits and other organizations," said Michelle Apodaca, director of the offices of the chairman, CEO, COO, and CFO. "There is a lot of trash talking within Deckers to see who can volunteer the most hours," Apodaca said with a laugh. "We've been blessed in this company, and we all realize this is our time to give back." Deckers employees also focus on giving back to the communities in and near its international offices, where employees volunteer on behalf of local causes in such cities as London, Paris, Beijing, and Hong Kong.

Employees have responded to the company's volunteer incentives in a big way, volunteering over 8,000 hours globally and nearly 6,000 hours locally since 2010. Many have even become board members of various local charities. Martinez, for example, sits on the board of directors for the Academy of Healing Arts; Mark Heintz, the Deckers director of corporate responsibility, is a member of

the Environmental Defense Center; Jessica Buttimer, chief brand officer, is a board member of the Santa Barbara Natural History Museum; Graciela Montgomery, senior vice president of human resources, sits on the board at the Lobero Theatre; and Yul Vanek, vice president of information technology, is a member of the finance committee and a vice chair on the board of directors at the Santa Barbara Zoo.

The company has even created an ongoing challenge it calls the "Good Games," according to Ariana Arcenas-Utley, corporate responsibility & sustainability specialist. The company is divided into 12 teams, which compete internally to see which team can log

the most volunteer hours. "Whenever we sponsor events for charity it builds morale," she said. "We even set up a 'speed dating' event each year with our employees and a variety of charities so the employees can talk to all the charities in a short time to learn more and decide where they want to volunteer. We also have an annual shoe drive where we send thousands of pairs of shoes to people in need."

Deckers has become so well known for its volunteers that organizations now call the company for help. The company has donated nearly $1.5 million to local charities and is a sponsor of the Santa Barbara Zoo, the Museum of Natural History, the Boys and Girls Club and Special Olympics of Santa Barbara, the Food Bank, Kids Helping Kids, Habitat for Humanity, Unity Shoppe, Girls Inc., and others.

"We get about 50 requests per week from charities," said Apodaca. "We try to help wherever we can. Our employees love the fact that this company is so giving and that the entire Santa Barbara community—as well as the other commuties around the globe in which we operate our businesses— benefit from all of our efforts. It's very rewarding for all of us."

495-A South Fairview Avenue
Santa Barbara, CA 93117
(805) 967-7611

Maps.com
Leading the Way to New Digital Opportunities

Digital technology may be changing the way the company does business, but the future appears robust for Goleta-based Maps.com. One thing remains constant: people love maps.

"We are defining maps for the 21st century," said John Glanville, who bought the company in 2012 and chairs the board of directors. "We have transitioned into a multidimensional map-printing company, producing maps in every conceivable format, from mobile apps and interactive textbooks to smart phone content and printed maps of all types."

The fact that the 37-employee firm now goes by its URL indicates the direction in which Glanville is taking the company. "Location-based services and products are critical to nearly every business, industry, institution, government, and individual," he said. "Where Maps.com differentiates itself from Google, Apple, and other virtual map providers is in the quality of our maps. Making great maps isn't easy. But I feel we are the best in the business."

National Geographic, Rand McNally, and many other firms rely on Maps.com to print and ship their maps. Annually, more than 150,000 retail customers purchase products from the Maps.com website, and another 500,000 orders come from governments, businesses, and educational textbook companies.

Maps.com employs an eclectic workforce, from cartographers to graphic designers, software engineers, and salespeople.

"Each of our cartographers is an artist," said Sarah Sinclair, president

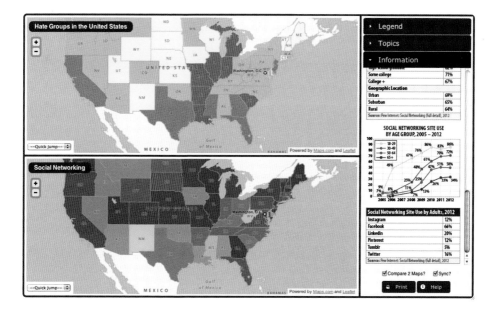

Some college	71%	
College +	67%	
Geographic Location		
Urban	69%	
Suburban	65%	
Rural	64%	

Source: Pew Internet: Social Networking (full detail), 2012

SOCIAL NETWORKING SITE USE BY AGE GROUP, 2005 – 2012

Social Networking Site Use by Adults, 2012

Instagram	12%
Facebook	66%
LinkedIn	20%
Pinterest	12%
Tumblr	5%
Twitter	16%

Source: Pew Internet: Social Networking (full detail), 2012

and CEO. "That gives us a huge edge in quality."

Glanville, a highly successful technology investor from Montecito, names several employees as being critical to the company's success: Sarah Sinclair, president and CEO; Tina Sicre Miller, executive vice president and COO; Paul Chapman, vice president of sales; Loraine Klotz, sales director; Bennett Moe, director of business development; Rob Burns, director of marketing; Bryan Conant, director of mapping services; Amy Pasko, director of information technology; Anne Messner, CFO; and Bill Spicer, eCommerce manager.

The future includes educational opportunities to "tell great stories with great maps," according to Sinclair, as interactive and customized visual learning, which usually involve maps, becomes increasingly popular. "Maps are an integral part of understanding the world around us," said Glanville. "It is part of our DNA. It's one of the reasons people love maps."

www.maps.com

"We are defining maps for the 21st century."

To find out how to include your organization in the 2014 edition of *Santa Barbara Community Builders*, or to suggest an organization, business, or individual that should be included, please email jeff@sbcommunitybuilders.com or see www.sbcommunitybuilders.com.